OUT OF THE SHADOWS

OUT OF THE SHADOWS

MY LIFE OF VIOLENCE IN AND OUT OF THE RING

DOMINIC NEGUS
WITH IVAN SAGE

JOHN BLAKE

Published by John Blake Publishing Ltd,
3 Bramber Court, 2 Bramber Road,
London W14 9PB, UK

www.blake.co.uk

First published in hardback in 2007

ISBN: 978-1-84454-354-0

British Library Cataloguing-in-Publication Data:

A catalogue record for this book is available from the British Library.

Design by www.envydesign.co.uk

Printed in Great Britain by CPD, Wales

1 3 5 7 9 10 8 6 4 2

Papers used by John Blake Publishing are natural, recyclable products
made from wood grown in sustainable forests. The manufacturing
processes conform to the environmental regulations of the country
of origin.

Every effort has been made to contact the relevant copyright holders.
Any omission is inadvertent; we would be grateful if the appropriate
people could contact us.

To my Dad
Cyril Walter Negus
The only man I've ever been in awe of
RIP

CONTENTS

TRIBUTES TO DOMINIC NEGUS

Too many people think Big Dom is just that... a Big Dom, another Essex lump with a crew cut. They are wrong. I've known Dom for many, many years. I've seen him box as an amateur and fight as a pro on both sides of the legal divide. And, I've seen him at night, no rules, no gloves, no prize money or trophy. I've seen him in hopeless causes, even boxing matches and some nasty affairs.

Dominic Negus is not easy to understand and I don't mean his accent. He's a mixture of right and wrong and nine-pound hammers and jokes. A mixture of heart and tears.

Too many people assume they know too much about people like Dominic. But then again, that is the way things work when you have a reputation and it's a reputation that has not been given away for nothing.

There are so many things that I never knew about Dominic and I thought that I knew him well. I was wrong. His book changed it for me. I know him better now and I like him even more.

Steve Bunce, BBC Sport boxing pundit,
writer, broadcaster and journalist

Dominic Negus is what unlicensed boxing is all about – he never picked his opponents or ever gave a monkey's about who he fought. Dominic would fight whoever was put in front of him.

Roy 'Pretty Boy' Shaw, former bare-knuckle
fighter and unlicensed boxing champion

Dominic's quite a character. The first time I met him was when I brought him in to spar with Scott Welch who was preparing for a world title fight. As Dominic entered the gym I said: 'Nice to meet you. How many rounds do you think you can do?' Dominic looked at Scott and said to me: 'Well, that rather depends on how many *he* can do!' A typical Dominic line.

Jim McDonnell, boxing trainer and former
undefeated European featherweight champion

Dominic is a colourful character. He was interesting to work with and he's packed a lot into his life.

Frank Maloney, boxing promoter

x

I first met professional boxer Dominic 'The Milky Bar Kid' Negus when he signed for my brother Frank. I remember telling Frank at the time what a tough kid he was. I like Dominic, he's an okay guy – a genuine fella who backs up what he says.

Eugene Maloney, boxing promoter, manager and trainer

First and foremost, Dominic is a friend. Secondly, he is a true grit fighter both in and out of the ring. Lastly, if I was in a tight spot, I can't think of anyone I'd rather have on my side.

Steve Holdsworth, writer and broadcaster

Dominic's a really good bloke – a bloke you'd want in your corner rather than the opposite one!

Spencer Oliver, Sky Television boxing commentator and former European super bantamweight champion

Dominic's a top, top bloke – a close friend. He's one of the few people I can count on. What a character. He's the type of guy fighters need to have around them.

Dave Coldwell, boxing promoter

I first heard of Dominic when he fought Audley Harrison. Then, when I met him, I thought what a great guy he was. He's got a lot of heart and he's a great gentleman with it.

Matt Skelton, British and Commonwealth
heavyweight champion

Dominic Negus is a colourful character. In the ring or on the street you know exactly what you will get from him – no nonsense, just 100 per cent commitment. My kind of bloke.

Barry Hearn, boxing promoter

Dominic boxed for my organisation for two years and became the IBA heavyweight world champion. Pound for pound Dominic is one of the best heavyweights out there. A true gladiator.

Alan Mortlock, president of the Independent Boxing Association

Dom is a gentleman with good family values. I respect him because he doesn't just talk the talk, he can walk the walk and, believe me, that's a walk you wouldn't want to take with Mr Negus. He's a nice bloke – until it's time not to be – and that's when it's time to fuck off! When Dom climbs into the ring he goes to work like a suit goes to the office. Meeting Dom in the ring was a night's work I never really fancied!

Phil Soundy, IBA British cruiserweight title contender

Tributes for Dominic Negus

Dom is an old hand in the game and is still the benchmark I'm aiming to emulate within the unlicensed world. He's still a respected boxer within the professional ranks. He's far from being an angel but, in my opinion, he's a rough diamond who, since becoming a father, decided to polish his edges a little more.

I wish him and his family all the best for the future. I'm also pissed off he packed the game in as I would have liked another shot at him!

Jeff Temperley, Dominic's unlicensed IBA world heavyweight title opponent

I've known Dominic for a number of years now. Our paths have often crossed in the boxing world and I've always had the highest respect for him and found him to be a man of his word. More recently, since Dominic became a family man, I have become very close to him and found him to be a very good, loyal and thoughtful friend. I wish him and his family all the best for the future.

Ray Coleman, Dominic's boxing sponsor

I would love to able to put into words how I feel about Dominic. However, words would not or could not do the man justice. How does one explain how one feels about another person, a new-found friend who, literally, came into my heart from Out of the Shadows. Dominic is a man I trust implacably and would go to battle for any time if need be. I believe Dominic is an honourable man. I am proud to be associated with him and I am extremely honoured to be able to call him my friend.

Ron Nash, vice president Millennium Events Inc,
America and Australia

FOREWORD

by Joe Egan

(Four times Irish boxing champion)

Dominic Negus is a man amongst men. He's a man I'm glad is on my side.

He's a man I am proud to call my friend; a man who was a great ambassador for boxing; a man devoted to his family; a man with a great sense of humour; a man as hard as nails.

Dominic is a man I'm glad I never had to fight!

Former world heavyweight champion Mike Tyson once nicknamed me the 'Toughest White Man on the Planet'.

Well, if such a title really existed, Dominic would be a contender without a shadow of doubt.

INTRODUCTION
by Ivan Sage

My friendship with boxer Dominic Negus began ten years ago and, since the BBC's fly-on-the-wall documentary *Underground Britain: Hard Man* – which revealed Dominic's life as an uncompromising debt collector – was screened, and in the light of him being arrested in connection with an armed kidnapping, our relationship, unsurprisingly, has prompted some raised eyebrows both from family and friends.

Undoubtedly, Dominic comes with some heavy baggage. He's a complex character who can be either witty and charming, or frightening and brutal. Dominic lives, or should I say lived, in a world where violence is the common currency; a world where rigid codes of behaviour – completely alien to most right-minded people – must at all times be adhered to.

Anyone breaking the unwritten rules in such a shadowy world could easily find themselves in dire trouble – or even treading that fine line between life or death. Justice in this world can be frighteningly brutal.

In short, our two worlds could hardly be more different. Yet, through my frequent contact with him over the past few years as a newspaper boxing correspondent, I have always found Dominic to be a bubbly and helpful subject – even though he's been somewhat elusive at times! As it turns out, that has probably been out of necessity, bearing in mind the situations he has found himself in on occasions. I guess Dominic really came to the wider public's attention when he fought Olympic gold medal winner Audley Harrison in July 2002 at Wembley Arena. I spent three hours prior to that contest with Dominic in his dressing room. He was chilling out, listening to music, and laughing and joking with his trainer Lenny Butcher and well-wishers, while a doctor, appointed by the British Boxing Board of Control, watched his every move, just in case he should succumb to the temptation of taking a performance-enhancing substance prior to the fight.

Throughout the contest, I enjoyed a prime position with Lenny in Dominic's corner. As ever, Dominic was confident he could beat Harrison just by relying on his natural strength and ability. However, the contest will long be remembered for the moment when Harrison clubbed Dominic on the side of the head while he was on one knee in the fourth round. Incensed by

Introduction

Harrison's obvious breach of etiquette, Dominic completely lost his cool. He spat out his gumshield, jumped up to remonstrate with Harrison, then head-butted him in full view of everyone, television cameras included. If ever there was a moment to publicly reveal the beast within Dominic, this was it, and he was certainly fortunate not to have been disqualified there and then. The furore over his conduct did him few favours with the media – he lost on points too – but far worse was to follow. Weeks later, the British Boxing Board of Control handed Dominic a fine and an indefinite ban after traces of the metabolite of the anabolic steroid Stananozol were found in a urine sample taken prior to the contest.

True to form, Dominic ignored the British Boxing Board of Control's penalties. He has since packed out arenas while fighting in the unlicensed side of the sport. He was crowned the IBA's world heavyweight champion in November 2005. The following month he won the Roy Shaw title and, immediately afterwards, announced his ring retirement.

What follows is a picture of a man with a history steeped in violence, a man who now faces the biggest and most important fight of his life.

This is his story.

Chapter One

THE AXE ATTACK

'**D**OMINIIIIIIIIC, *yaaaaaaaaaaaaaaaaaaah* – *we've come for you!*'

It was April 2004 in the Five Star gymnasium in Harold Hill on the outskirts of London. I was just taking off my top in the changing room, getting ready to go into a training and sparring session in preparation for my IBA heavyweight world title contest against some ugly German geezer in Braintree.

That may sound grand but this contest was for a little-recognised unlicensed title. By now, my days as a bona fide professional boxer under the umbrella of the British Boxing Board of Control were over. I was subject to an indefinite ban from the sport after traces of a steroid had been found in my urine in the wake of my controversial contest against British Olympic

1

golden boy Audley Harrison at Wembley in July 2002 – but more about that later.

Back to the changing rooms. On hearing the commotion, I swung around just in time to see three fellas bursting in. All three had their heads covered with plastic shopping bags with holes cut out for their eyes. Seeing them coming towards me in such a threatening manner was quite a surreal experience and, when I noticed that the smallest fella had a gun, well, to be honest, it scared the shit out of me.

Ever the diplomat, I shouted at him: 'What are you gonna do with that you little cunt?' and then, BANG, I was going over. What's going on? I wondered as I found myself halfway down to the floor. Well, while I'd been watching the little sod with the shooter, his mate – let's call him Big Lump – had got behind me and clobbered me on the back of the head with an axe.

Now, for various reasons, which will become apparent later, this was a time in my life when my mind was all over the place. The paranoia I had been experiencing initially caused me to believe my attackers were friends of mine, Paul, Matty and Mark, particularly as they were of a similar build. Fuckin' hell, I thought, I've got some good mates here!

But this was no time to let my mind wander, I was in big trouble, that much even I was aware of. I shouted out; 'I know who you are, what's this all about?' But my attackers had obviously not visited me for a chat. I'd got a reputation for being a hard man, but I was getting done over here. I was in shock, then it was fear... and then I got the right hump – and, as many have found to their cost in the past, it really isn't a good idea to wind me up!

I realised there was no way I could let them take me anywhere. Had they managed that I knew it would have been a one-way ticket. I jumped up to my feet. Everything was happening so quickly but I was aware of thinking it was raining. Of course, being inside, it wasn't rain – the axe wound on the back of my head was spurting blood upwards – just like those squirters that clean car windscreens. The blood was pumping out fast, over the top of my head, and dropping onto my face.

Big Lump came at me again, trying to strike me again with the axe. I had to get hold of that axe. Instinctively, I tried to grab it as it came rushing down towards me. As a result, my right hand was sliced wide open. Somehow, despite the injury, I managed to hold on to the axe and wouldn't let it go. With my other hand, I grabbed Big Lump around the throat.

'You big cunt!' I roared. Big Lump screamed out to his other mate who had, until then, been occupying his time rather productively by whacking me with a baseball bat. 'Don't just fuckin' stand there, *DO* something!' then WHACK, the baseball bat made full contact with my raised left forearm as I tried to protect my head.

Of course, during the proceedings there had been quite a bit of noise emanating from the changing room. Outside, in the gym, my trainer Lenny Butcher was quite unaware of exactly what was going on and had assumed my raised voice meant I was yelling at someone down the phone, a not uncommon occurrence bearing in mind my sideline as an 'unofficial' debt collector.

Nevertheless, when Lenny opened the changing room door he found himself staring down the barrel of a shooter and, quite reasonably, he wasn't too happy. As the little geezer advanced towards him, Lenny, thinking quickly, shut the door in his face, bolted it and tried to hold it shut. 'Do you want some?' yelled the gunman through the door at him. Obviously, Lenny didn't. He shouted out to Wolfie (Adam Wolf), a young boxer who had been working out in the gym, to go and get the Old Bill. Then Lenny made a break for it. Meanwhile, the gunman managed to get through the door and went looking for Lenny but, thankfully, Lenny managed to give him the slip.

Back in the changing room, Big Lump's mate was still swinging at me with the baseball bat. I stepped back and instinctively adopted a boxing stance. As he came at me again with the bat I made a grab for it. Worryingly, because of the deep cut already inflicted, I realised my hand wasn't working properly but, somehow, I managed to pull the bat towards me and, not willing to relinquish possession, he came forward with it. As soon as he was in range I delivered a karate chop to his neck and he went flying onto the floor. I should point out I'm a boxer and not exactly Bruce Lee or Steven Seagal, but I'd been getting badly hurt. This was desperation. I was fighting for my life.

Holding grimly onto the bat, I found myself backed up to the toilet cubicle. Psyching myself up, I began to whack the bat noisily against the cubicle. Outnumbered and bleeding profusely, I had to bullshit my way out of this situation. 'Come on then, do you want it? Come on, I'm ready!' All this time I had been expecting to hear a loud bang and a burning sensation. A couple of my associates had previously told me how it felt to be shot. All the same, I had to try to concentrate on the situation as it presented itself at the time. The guy was on the floor, screaming, 'Don't hit me, don't hit me!' Big Lump yelled to him, 'Use the gas, squirt him, squirt him!' By now, the gunman had given up looking for Lenny and had rejoined his colleagues. Seconds later I found myself having CS gas and ammonia sprayed over me. I had to back away. I had ammonia on my clothes and I certainly didn't want it on my face. For some reason I found myself yelling at them, 'What do you think you're doing, that ain't the way to do it!'

In the distance, the sound of the Old Bill hurrying to the scene could be heard. 'Let's go, let's go!' yelled Big Lump and, with that, they legged it. By now, I was in a bad way. I was holding the bat and watched through the window as the three fellas ran outside, jumped into their car and pissed off. I was thinking is that it?

Lenny came running back into the gym. 'Dom, Dom, I'm so sorry,' he said. He was feeling bad that he hadn't hung around, but what the hell was he supposed to do when he had a shooter pointing at his head?

'Look, Lenny,' I said, '*I'm* sorry. Look at the state of the gym. There's claret everywhere, who's gonna clean that lot up?'

But Lenny was more worried about me. He sat me down. 'I'm alright,' I insisted. 'Can I go home?' There was no way that would have been possible as blood was still spurting from the head wound. I'd already lost an awful lot of claret and, by now, Lenny had towels wrapped tightly around the cuts to my hands and arms. Lenny insisted I had to go to hospital, but I was telling him to fuck off, no way was I going into any hospital.

Suddenly, this guy came through the door. Still a bit jumpy, I asked him, 'Who the fuck are you?'

'I'm a copper,' he replied. I stood there, baseball bat still in my hand. Seconds later there were Old Bill everywhere and an ambulance turned up. A medic, seeing the extent of my injuries, told me I had to get onto a stretcher. I refused. 'You've got to,' he said. 'You've lost a lot of blood and there's loads more still pumping out of your head.' He was only doing his job, but I told him, 'Look, I've had three geezers in here tonight trying to lay me down and they couldn't, so I ain't gonna lay down for you!'

I suppose the attack, in some ways at least, did me some good. Perhaps it was good to have been on the receiving end for a change because it made me realise exactly what I'd been dishing out to other people for so long.

I deserved it. It became the turning point of my life. My 'Road to Damascus' experience if you like. It made me realise that, if I couldn't take it, then I'm not a man. I could so easily have been killed that night and the attack had been the culmination of a downward spiral my life had taken over the preceding months. After experiencing the physical and mental injuries of the attack and its consequences, I had, not for the first time in my life, reached rock bottom.

From that point onwards, the only way to go was up.

Chapter Two

EARLY DAYS

I've made a lot of mistakes in my life. Perhaps the person people see isn't the real me. Perhaps writing this book will help me to understand why I have done some of the really bad things I've done in the past. I want a second chance. People like me don't often get that. People only see Dom the fighter, Dom the doorman, Dom the hard man. I'm sure some people probably think I haven't even got a brain.

Yet one of my mates told me recently that I'm probably one of the most sensitive people he's ever known. It's just that I get so upset over silly things.

How would I describe myself? Very misunderstood. Deep down, I know I can be a nice guy. But I can't hide from my past. I want this book to be like an open apology to people as well. It doesn't matter what I've said. After what I've done to some people, me saying sorry won't mean anything. Perhaps this is just me trying to clear my conscience.

There are a lot of people I've upset or hurt. But recently, something happened to make me realise just how much of an effect my actions must have had on others. This guy came up to me, asking for my advice. He was a grown man – as big as me he was – and he was crying his eyes out.

The guy knew I moonlighted by collecting debts – without the paperwork if you know what I mean – and he'd got into trouble because he'd got behind with paying his rent to his landlord. He'd been told to expect someone to come knocking on his door to 'persuade' him to pay up. He thought that the someone in question could be me and he was really worried about what I might be thinking of doing to him.

That really got to me because I know what I've done to people like him. It's the fear of what *might* happen. In most cases physical pain fades. Mental pain? Well, it doesn't.

When I was attacked in the changing rooms it wasn't the physical pain that caused most of my problems – but that's not to say I'm inviting them to come back for another go! No, it was more the paranoia I experienced afterwards. Suddenly, I could really relate to that guy asking for my advice.

I'm not devoid of any feeling for others. A while back I met this gay fella called Richard in a bar. I'd seen him there a number of times, so I knew him a bit.

A lot of people there didn't really like him because he's a poof, but he's nice enough. Richard came up to me asking me to loan him some cash. He'd heard I sometimes had a bit to lend, but my rates weren't exactly like Barclays. Normally, I'd say yes because I knew I'd always get my money back. People often borrowed money off me when they couldn't get it from anyone else. If I lent out a grand, I'd want two grand back in a month. That's how it was.

Richard was crying, really upset because he was missing his family in South Africa. He was desperate to go back to visit them. I told him it wouldn't make sense for him to borrow money off me. 'My rates are far too dear for you. I know you're bent but we get on okay and I don't want to fall out with you. If you can't pay it back, believe me, I would.'

I left him in the bar and went outside. I walked up the street to a travel agent's and handed over £900 for tickets to and from South Africa. Then I returned to the bar. By now Richard had left, but I found him a little way down the street, just outside a supermarket. 'Oi, you big poof!' I shouted. 'I've got something for you.' I gave him the envelope containing the tickets and returned, once again, to the bar. Meanwhile, Richard had opened the envelope and found the tickets. He followed me into the bar. I told him he should sort things out with his boyfriend because I didn't want him getting the wrong idea and thinking I was moving in on Richard. I told him that he should piss off to South Africa for a couple of weeks.

11

Richard was still crying and told me he couldn't afford to pay me back, but I told him not to bother. I thought it was nice that someone missed their family so much and the fact that, for a change, I could do something nice for someone else and that made me feel good.

The trouble was, my good deed caused me to have a bit of a falling out with a friend of mine who I'd lent £500. When I went to collect he asked why I wanted it back if I could afford to give a poof £900 for an airline ticket. I told him it was *my* money and that if I took the £500 off him there and then and burned it, that's up to me. I made him pay up.

I guess I can't really apologise to most people I've hurt. Why should they accept my apologies for what I've done? I guess I just want them to realise it was nothing personal – just business that came my way during what I now call 'my lost years'.

Boxing aside, a lot of my true friends don't see me as an aggressive person. I'm usually laughing and joking around – well, at least 95 per cent of the time. But it's the other 5 per cent. That used to be so different. That said, I never used to take liberties with people who were not in that sort of circle. They all knew what they were up to, and the consequences of me turning up at their doors. If I turned up they knew they'd fucked up big time somewhere along the line – they hadn't played the game. It's been the same scenario for years, but now I'm tired of it. I know I have a short fuse but, nowadays, it takes so much more to trigger it off.

A friend who runs a gym shop told me I had to write this book because, 'the stories you come up with are amazing'. I told him they were all true. 'That's just it,' he replied, 'And everyone around here knows it.'

These days I prefer to be at home with my partner Nichola, baby Annabella and stepdaughter Lauren. If I go out now, it's just for a couple of Guinnesses, then I want to be back home with Nic and the kids because, after a certain time around these parts, that's when the idiots come out, and I just can't be around those sort of people any more.

I'm well-known – particularly in Essex and the Greater London area – and, if I go into the arena, it's like I'm expected to perform. Look, I'm no angel. I've done a bit of alcohol and a bit of coke – that's how my life was, but not any more. If I go out for a drink now, I prefer a quiet little pub where I can meet my mates – real people with nine-to-five jobs. Grafters. Good people.

Just recently, boxer Mike Tyson flew to Britain for a series of speaking engagements and to sign copies of four-times Irish amateur champion Joe Egan's new biography. I was invited to go along to see them. A couple of old faces noticed me and tried to gee me up a bit, telling me how much I'd changed. So what? I thought. These were the guys who, when everything in my life went down the toilet, didn't want to know, even though I'd done the business for them when they wanted loans repaid.

Maybe I've just got wiser. These days, I've got so much more to lose.

Although I've always loved my boxing, I was a single guy when I was on the professional circuit. Now, when I look at my baby, I just think I want to be with her. I want to be there when she starts talking properly. I want to be there for her first day at school. I want to be part of every aspect of her life.

When I look back at some of the people I know really well who are in and out of prison, well, that's the life they've chosen and I don't want to be part of that world anymore. I've had my share of scrapes and aggro and I know there are a lot of people out there who are sure I cannot change. All I can ask is that they just give me a chance to prove I can.

So, here it is, this is my story, the story of fighting back against all the demons that have blighted my life and people around me. It's a bumpy ride, but here goes...

Let's start at the beginning. Dominic Antony Negus was born at Bethnal Green Hospital on 28 July 1970, a brother for two-year-old Freddy. Some years previously, my mum, Stella Tianni, met and married Cyril Walter Negus, a man 20 years her senior. Dad was 50 when I was born.

Dad was in the print. He was a proper grafter who never took a day off work in his life. He worked on the reels in Grays Inn Road, London, on *The Times* newspaper. Dad worked nights. In fact, I can never remember a time when he ever played with Freddy or me. Not football or anything. That was hardly surprising because he used to leave our three-bedroomed semi-detached home in Greenstead Avenue, Woodford, at half past six each evening and never returned until four the following morning, so he was always knackered.

We had a nice home, I suppose. This part of Woodford might not have been top notch, but it was a decent area all the same. Our house had a garage to the side, and Dad had an aviary in the back garden. While we were younger, Freddy and me kept rabbits and guinea pigs.

Dad was very old-fashioned in a lot of ways. We never got any hugs from him, which was a shame because even now, as big as I am, I still like a cuddle. But he was never cold towards us. Just old-school. Don't forget, by the time I was 10, he was 60. It was such a big age difference.

Mum, on the other hand, was far more affectionate towards us, but she wasn't too soft not to give us a slap if ever we deserved it. Mum used to work at the Claybury Hospital, Woodford Bridge, as a nurse and, later in life, as a cleaner. She also did some waitressing in The George, a pub in South Woodford.

Whenever he went off to work, Dad would always tell Freddy and me to be good for our mother. 'Of course,' we'd say but, in truth, as soon as he'd gone we'd be little bastards! To stop us Mum would say 'I'll tell your father!' or 'wait till your father gets home!' I can remember a day Freddy and me came a cropper, though. One summer's Sunday afternoon we were supposed to be having a bath. We had our towels wrapped around us and started mucking about. As Dad left, he told us to behave. We quietened down a bit, but only until we heard the front door shut and then it was bedlam. We were bouncing up and down on the couch and Mum was getting really angry with us. We just laughed at her. Trouble was, amid all the commotion, we hadn't heard the key in the front door. Dad came back in and gave us a right hiding.

I reacted the way I've always reacted to pain ever since. I refused to show it. I gritted my teeth. No way was I going to cry in front of my old man like Freddy was. Mind you, the moment I was alone, I cried my eyes out!

Freddy and I promised not to do it again, but Dad told us our promises meant nothing. They were empty. Well, that may have been the case with Freddy but, as far as I'm concerned, my promise was my bond, and it always has been.

I wouldn't say Freddy was a spoilt kid, but he'd kick up quite a stink sometimes, wanting this or that but then, I suppose, he did pave the way for me a bit. If he wanted to go out, Mum and Dad might have thought he was too young but, in some ways, when he was allowed out, he made it easier for me to do what I wanted to because, if he broke the rules, I'd say 'if he can do it, why can't I?' Dad's usual answer was, 'When you're old enough to get a job and earn your own money, you can,' which was one of the reasons I couldn't wait to leave school at the age of 15.

My first experience of schooling was at St Anthony's

Catholic Infant School in Woodford High Road. I didn't exactly get expelled but, when Mum and Dad transferred Freddy to the nearby Wood Bridge School, St Anthony's asked them if they'd send me there with him too as I'd been such a little bastard. In fact, I was always getting caned for mucking about or play fighting. Nothing really serious, but Catholic schools tend to be very strict. If ever I mucked about in PE I'd get the slipper. Looking back, I reckon I was no more than a lovable rogue, a bit cheeky, that's all.

I was nine when I left St Anthony's. I found myself spending the next year at Ray Lodge, a junior school in Snakes Lane, Woodford, where, by all accounts, I was always in some sort of trouble. I hated it there because, coming from a Catholic school background, I was given a rough welcome. That's when I first started to find myself getting involved in a few fights. It was then I realised that, up to a point, I could look after myself.

It didn't last. When I later became a pupil at Wood Bridge High School I was bullied, both verbally and physically, by the older kids. It was a hard school. A lot of the kids there were rejects from other schools in the area and, being fat and wearing glasses, I was an obvious target for those who wanted to show off.

Looking back, I realise now that I wasted too much time during my school years. I was always trying to make the other kids laugh rather than concentrating on my studies. I wasn't too bad academically, although in the early days I did have some difficulties with reading and writing. Spelling and maths – well, I was shit at those, but I reckon I was just a typical lad. My reports too often had the comment 'Dominic could do much better if he were to concentrate'.

I really hated it at Wood Bridge. I could hardly wait to leave the place, mainly I suppose, because of the bullying I was experiencing at that time and, although I would have liked to have stayed away at times, Dad was more of the opinion that I had to go to school. That was the way it should be – you go to school and, after that, you go to work. That's the way he grew up so Freddy and me should do the same.

I suppose my main circle of friends at the time were Jason Burton – who I'm still in touch with – Mark Lucas, Richard Glanville and Gary 'Foggy' Elgar. We used to love riding around Woodford on our bikes or going fishing down the river Roding.

Our next-door neighbours, Dave and Barbara Jones, had three kids – Paul, Ian and Sarah. Paul was my age, Ian was a couple of years older and I think Sarah was a bit younger. We were always hanging about together. Their parents became known to Freddy and me as Aunty Barbara and Uncle Dave – which was the old-fashioned and respectful way Mum and Dad had taught us both to address older friends of the family.

Paul, Ian and me would often go camping. We were in the cubs. I loved it, even though our group were a bit, shall we say, 'naughty'. I remember one kid getting a broken arm as the result of one of the fights.

At the time I was really into books and films,

particularly anything to do with *Star Wars*. In fact, I collected – or I should say nicked – nearly all the *Star Wars* figures that were so popular with youngsters at the time.

We used to play all sorts of games and pranks, one of which was Knock Down Ginger, when you knock on people's doors and leg it before they answer. We did that a lot. Trouble was, because I was the fat one, I couldn't run off as fast as the others and I often got caught.

It wasn't all play though. I had three jobs – a paper round, and, after school, I would go along to a local butcher's shop where I was paid a pittance to clean up. I also worked Saturdays and Sundays for a couple of years, stacking up the shelves in a supermarket. Again, only for silly money. Nevertheless, it still provided me with that little bit of extra cash so I could go out and buy even more *Star Wars* figures and other sci-fi bits and pieces.

By the time I was at Wood Bridge High, Dad had retired. If any of the kids wanted to bunk off school, our home was the meeting place. Mum was usually out at work, but Dad didn't mind because he reckoned it was better we were there rather than hanging around the estate. Of course there was always the chance someone would come knocking to find out why we were not at school but Dad had made a gate at the bottom of our garden which led into our neighbours' garden, so I always knew I could nip through there in plenty of time before anyone found me out.

Freddy and me had a great childhood. Okay, there wasn't a lot of money around but we always had shoes on our feet and a decent meal on the table. In fact, Mum was what I'd call a typical Italian woman. She always insisted we sat at the dinner table for our meals and that everything had to be done just right.

What we lacked as far as material things were concerned was more than made up for by the laughs we had together. It was a very happy household. So often we hear people blaming their past for the wrongs in their current life but, in truth, I could never do that. My mum was great with us. So was Dad – even if we did go short on cuddles.

Chapter Three
THE WORM TURNS

Violence has played a huge part in my life, both on a professional basis and otherwise. Although there had been plenty of scraps at school there was never anything too serious. That is, not until I was nearly 11 years old.

It was just before the summer holidays. Freddy and me were sitting with Ian and Paul, reading our comics on their front porch. After a while, about eight older kids from the nearby Broadmead Estate walked past. One of them was a black kid and I knew he was a bit handy. 'Look at that fat cunt,' he said, pointing directly at me. 'Piss off nig-nog,' I replied, which, looking back, wasn't such a good idea as they came storming over to us. The black kid came right up to me. I put my hands up to protect myself but I wasn't quick enough and he kicked me right in the mouth. My head hit the floor with a crack and then one of them stamped on it. I'll always remember I had what looked like a big Reebok-style imprint on my head for days and my glasses were smashed. I managed to get up to try to defend myself but I ended up getting a good hiding. Then they just walked away. Freddy, Ian and Paul were crying because they hadn't been able to help me but there was nothing really that they could have done, otherwise they'd have got beaten up too.

I went home and found Dad in the garage. Obviously, he wanted to know what had happened and all I could say was, 'Why did it have to be me? I hate being fat.' Dad went mad and wanted to go after them but I insisted he didn't because I was worried they'd set on him too – even though he'd previously been an undefeated welterweight champion in his Army years.

It took me about a week to recover from the injuries I sustained that day. Looking in the mirror I looked like the Elephant Man. I was determined that would never happen to me again.

I guess I was about 11 years old when I first saw a live boxing contest. Mum and Dad took me to St James Hawkey Hall in Woodford for a Garden City Boxing Club dinner event. There was a special bout that night featuring Colin McMillan, a lad roughly my age from Barking, who went on to win the British, Commonwealth and world featherweight titles. I thought it was great. I can't remember who he was fighting that night, but Colin was a junior champion at the time and he was a really nice kid.

About a year later, when I was 12, Dad took me back to Garden City ABC – later known as Gator ABC – and I began learning to box there. Although, at first, I got right into it, at that stage in my life it wasn't something I particularly wanted to spend all my time doing. There were other interests, like hanging around with my mates, that I also wanted to do. I stuck at it for about a year but, even though I left, a seed had been planted in me that would play a big part in my later life.

Rachel Goldstraw. This was someone I really fancied. Trouble was, she was my English teacher and I was just a kid. And the feeling probably wasn't mutual because Miss Goldstraw decided I should write out an essay about what I wanted to do with my life as a punishment for larking about in class. As far as I was concerned, there was only one possibility. I wanted to be a professional boxer so I wrote about all the fitness training and dedication that would be needed to achieve that aim. When I had finished, Miss Goldstraw read my account to the class. One of the kids, Paul Kelly, started to take the mickey. 'You'll never be a boxer,' he said. Miss Goldstraw, though, was having none of it. 'See that boy there,' she said, pointing to me, 'that boy has got more gumption than you'll ever have!' Well, that really boosted my confidence.

I remember now how, on the last day of term before

the summer holiday, I bought her a Reader's Digest book as a thank you gift and jokingly asked her for a kiss as I handed it to her.

To my surprise she gave me a tiny peck on the cheek. I couldn't think about anything else through the holiday and, for once, I couldn't wait to get back to school. So much for childhood crushes.

Although I hated school, I did like some subjects. English for instance. I loved it. But, then again, Miss Goldstraw was the teacher! That aside, I reckon I got to be pretty good at writing essays. Other subjects I particularly enjoyed were woodwork and cookery and, after a while, I became quite good at both of them.

I wasn't the best as far as physical education was concerned which, bearing in mind I was to enjoy a successful boxing career later in life, may come as a surprise to some readers. No, I have to admit, most of the other kids were usually better at sports than I was because I was a bit of a dough boy at the time. I was reasonably good at rugby, and used my weight to my advantage as I smashed the smaller lads out of the way. I was useless at football and cricket. I didn't mind playing basketball – although I wasn't that good at it – while cross country wasn't too bad either. Trouble was, we used to have what you might describe as an A team – those who were pretty good at it – then there were the retards like me who made up the B team. That said, I would usually manage to come home in third or fourth place within our group.

But my time at school wasn't totally wasted. When I left I had acquired CSEs in English, Cookery, Woodwork and History. Oh, and computer studies – but only because I cheated. Most of the marks for this subject were counted from projects and homework and it probably won't surprise anyone that I wasn't really into homework. I found it easier to nick a friend's notes and pass them off as my own. It may not have been the right thing to do, but it did the trick!

Dad and I often used to listen to boxing on the radio. I particularly remember listening in June 1984 when Thomas Hearns took on the legendary Roberto 'Hands of Stone' Duran at Caesar's Palace in Las Vegas. What a fight. Hearns, who ended his career having secured world championships at five weights, was all over Duran in the first round, cutting him over the eye and putting him down to the canvas for the first time in ten years, then again just before the bell. Then, in the second round, Hearns finished the job with a right hook that sent Duran face down onto the canvas. He'd been knocked spark out so the referee never even bothered to count.

However, it wasn't until I was about 15 or 16 that I went back into the gym. By that time I had left school and had found work with a next-door neighbour, Steve Bedwell. Steve had a place in Leytonstone, a car body workshop and valeting company. I began working as a valeter for Steve and his business partner Frank Barry.

While working there I took every opportunity to

sneak into the bodyshop to watch the guys spraying cars. One of them, a Paddy, was one of the very best sprayers you'd ever be likely to see. Amazing. That gave me an urge to give it a go myself.

I saw an advert in the Job Centre for a trainee car sprayer at Castle Garage in Woodford High Road. I applied and went along to meet the guys who ran the business, Colin Cordingley and Andrew Craft. I sat in front of Colin and he asked me what made me think he should give me the job. 'Because I can do it, that's why. As long as I get the proper training I want this job.' Colin agreed I could start the following Monday.

I loved working on the cars and I became a good paint sprayer. I'm one of those people who, if I do something, I want to give it my best shot. I worked there for about three years all told, then moved on to work for Sierra Motors in Leytonstone. It was around this time I got into working the doors at bars and nightclubs to earn a little extra cash. A friend of mine, John Cronie, had a mate we called Mutt – real name Jim Hutton. Mutt was a big lad, about 19 at the time, and into bodybuilding. He also did door work. We started hanging around together and Mutt suggested I try my hand at door work too.

Mutt took me to the Top Guard offices in Queens Road, Buckhurst Hill. That's where I first met Kevin Camp and his brother John or, as I call him, Johnny Fast Hands. Kevin and Johnny looked after a lot of people, including American singer Alice Cooper. They were obviously good at their jobs and, after a while, I began working with them.

Kevin is of a similar build to me – as I am now – and, although he can look after himself okay, he isn't one of the top boys. He had a go at boxing on the unlicensed scene but was knocked out in the first round. I guess that shows that, even if you can look after yourself on the street, it doesn't necessarily mean you can do the business in the ring. You can play at football or golf, but you can't play at boxing.

Johnny Fast Hands is the same stamp as me and, as I've discovered over the years, he is such a loyal person. In fact, he is far more loyal than is good for him. A great fella who's been a great friend.

My first night's work was at the door of the Astoria nightclub on Charing Cross Road in London's city centre. My colleague that night assured me there was never any trouble there but, you've guessed it, that night it all kicked off. It was totally mad. Gang warfare in the foyer. I didn't really know what I should have been doing so I just got stuck in.

After my early days working the doors I knew I could handle myself in a punch-up. No doubt about that. I remember going into a pub in Woodford Bridge with a mate who was a bit older than me, about 21 I think. Back then I still had curly hair and glasses. All the herberts were in there. Three or four geezers in there thought they were a bit tasty and started digging us a bit. Then this geezer started taking the piss out of us. I went mad. I went over to him and kicked the table into his chest as he was getting off his stool. 'If you want a fight, let's have one,' I said. 'Oh shut up mate,' he said, backing off. My mate reckoned we could be in for some trouble later on, but I didn't think so.

Then Freddy turned up. His missus, Anita, was pregnant at the time. She reckoned Freddy knew there could be trouble and didn't want to leave him, although she didn't get out of the car. By this time there were about five of us, having been joined by two other mates, Jeff and Andre. However, as soon as we went outside, the other geezers were waiting for us and, suddenly, it all kicked off. One geezer jumped onto my back and had his arms round my neck and was trying to throttle me. I pushed back against a wall then nutted him, and that was it. A couple of others got cut lips and bloody noses. It didn't last long but now I knew for sure that I could have a real fight – and that felt *really* good.

Later, I began to work on a pretty regular basis on the doors of The Venue, a nightclub in New Cross. To this day, I reckon it's one of the best nightclubs I've ever worked in – an indie club where top bands like The Pixies, Carter USM, New Model Army, The Levellers and The Cure, would turn up to play. I reckon I worked at The Venue for about three years. I always loved the music there. I got to see the bands, had a good time, and got paid for it at the same time.

Trouble is, when clubbers are dancing to grunge music, it involves steaming into each other in the middle of the dance floor so it's hard to tell if and when anything is kicking off. You usually have to wait until the music stops. If they're still at it, it's a fight. The door staff had to stand on boxes to get a good view of what was going on or, sometimes, we'd be alerted by panic buttons.

I'd always be the first to go running up to the top floor when the panic button sounded, which used to concern my colleague Johnny Gardener who we called Big John. 'Never run, always walk up there,' he told me. 'You never know what you're getting into if you go rushing in. You could end up getting stabbed. On the other hand, if there's ten geezers up there having a good punch-up, what's the point of steaming in when they're still fresh? Give 'em enough time to tire themselves out and then you can pull 'em out.'

It was good advice. I'd often been too keen to get involved and had been making the job much harder than it needed to be. Big John has hardly changed since we first met – other than getting around four stone heavier! Like Johnny Fast Hands, Big John's loyalty is second to none.

One night Johnny Fast Hands was on the doors at The Astoria. Although it was my night off, I still went along for a night out. I was still a fledgling doorman, 19 years old, with curly hair and glasses. I guess I didn't really look the part. Travelling with me was a mate, Simon Andrews, who was rostered for duty that night. When we arrived, I left Johnny and Simon and went upstairs to enjoy the evening. After a while, however, although I didn't know him so well at the time, I decided to return downstairs for a chat with Johnny who, at that particular moment in time happened to be the only doorman on duty.

As I entered the foyer, I noticed a big coloured geezer scuffling with Johnny. Apparently, the management had told Johnny that no-one should be allowed to leave the premises as, moments before, some 'steamers' – people who jump over the bar to grab the takings in the tills – had been operating in the club. I hadn't had a lot of experience of doorwork but I decided to hang around, just in case Johnny needed a bit of back-up. At this point, another punter turned up and directed a comment at me which I didn't clearly hear.

'What's the matter with you?' I asked. He began to take the piss out of me, so I told him to fuck off.

'Oh, look at you,' he jeered, 'it's GI Joe with glasses!' That's when it all kicked off. Another geezer turned up, also wanting to leave the premises, but he was told he'd have to stay inside while the search for the steamer continued. That didn't please him, so he went for Johnny. Then there was an almighty tear-up which only ended when Johnny landed a peach of a punch directly onto the geezer's chin. He hit the wall, then slumped slowly to the floor. Within seconds, more blokes were jumping on top of Johnny, all kicking him and trying to knock lumps out of him. Well, I couldn't just stand around watching, so I waded in too.

Even now, Johnny recalls how he could feel the

weight of the pile of geezers on top of him being reduced bit by bit as I dragged them off him one by one and knocked them out.

It looked as if we had the situation under control but, unbeknown to me, someone else still had the intention of landing one on me. He'd raced down the stairs clutching a torch and was about to bring it down on the back of my head. It was another doorman called Archie. He'd thought I was one of the attackers because, being off duty, I wasn't wearing a uniform. Luckily, I spotted him just in time.

'Hey, Archie, it's me!!!'

He stopped in his tracks, then spotted my smashed glasses on the floor. He picked them up and handed them to me.

'Sorry Dom,' he said. 'I think these are yours!'

'Tel, I think I've killed a geezer!'

I was talking to Terry O'Neill, a doorman at a south London nightclub and, to be honest, I was shitting myself. I'd just run there as fast as I could from another nightclub where I sometimes worked the doors. In fact, this had been my evening off, but I had called at the club to see my colleagues, eight of whom had been working that night. Nearby, I noticed one of the punters, a real loon with a pink Mohican haircut. Apparently, he'd spent the best part of the evening being a real prick, screaming, shouting and annoying people. He'd already been chucked out of the club but, rather foolishly, he'd decided to return, this time brandishing a big lump of wood. For some reason, I decided to get involved.

I guess, at 19 years of age, I was keen to show that a curly haired geezer with glasses could handle himself should a problem arise. All my colleagues were very experienced doormen and I'm sure that, looking at me, few of them would have been convinced I could dig deep should the need arise. I guess that's what made me do what I did next. I needed to prove a point.

'Why don't you just go away mate?' I said to the loon.

'I ain't going anywhere,' he replied, adding, 'I'm gonna do you!'

'Oh yeah,' I replied. 'I suppose you'll be calling me GI Joe with glasses next too!'

'No, I'm not. You're a cunt!'

'Me, a cunt?'

'Yeah.'

I couldn't let him get away with that, particularly as all my colleagues had witnessed what had happened. I removed my glasses and handed them to Ian, one of the doormen. 'So,' I repeated, 'you reckon I'm a cunt?'

'Yeah.'

'What about him, then?' I asked, pointing at Ian. He glanced towards Ian. It was all I needed. BANG! I might only have weighed 14 stone, but I connected with his chin perfectly with a really hard right hook. He flew backwards, banging his head hard on the wall, before it made a sickening thud as it hit the floor. He was out cold. I was rather impressed with what I'd done, and felt sure the other doormen had been too.

Then I saw the blood.

There was lots of it seeping out from underneath his head onto the floor, and it was obvious I'd hurt him pretty badly. I decided it might be best not to hang about, particularly as it had not been my night for working. I retrieved my glasses from Ian and said, 'I think I'd better go.' I walked outside, then around the corner but, once out of view, I legged it as fast as I could until I reached Terry on the doors of the other nightclub.

No doubt about it. I was really worried. What if the loon was dead? It hardly bore thinking about. A while later I plucked up the courage to return to the club where the incident occurred. I was desperate to find out if the guy was okay. The lads told me that the noise of his head hitting the floor had alerted the club's manager and he'd come out front to find out what had been going on. An ambulance had been called and the loon, who was in quite a state, was taken away to the Accident and Emergency department of the local hospital for treatment.

The following evening it was my turn to do a shift at the club. When I arrived, I spotted the guy with the Mohican hanging around outside. At least he was still alive, I thought. I have to admit, I was very relieved.

'That's the geezer I bashed last night,' I told my colleague Simon. The geezer and I made eye contact.

'You alright mate?' I asked.

'Yeah, you?'

'Yeah.'

'Was I out of order last night?' he asked.

'What happened last night?' I replied innocently.

'I haven't a clue mate,' he replied. 'All I can remember is getting chucked out and waking up in hospital this morning with ten stitches in my head!'

A while later that evening, two friends, Dave and Dermott, who provided in-house security in the club, came up to me. They were grinning. 'Here, Dom, we heard you threw a corker of a right hand last night so we've got a present for you.' They passed me a resealable plastic sandwich bag.

'What's that?'

As I opened the bag I could see a clump of pink hair still attached to a large lump of skin and covered in blood. They'd found it stuck to the wall where the geezer had bumped his head and decided it would make a good souvenir of the incident. Sick bastards!

Nowadays, I can look back at this incident with wry amusement but, at the time, I'd been absolutely petrified I'd killed the fella.

So much for being a hard man.

When I was younger I used to go to Ilford Palais with my mates. The doormen there were pretty intimidating. Now I was one myself and, as a consequence, my self-confidence had risen sky high. I was a bit of a hunk too! That certainly helped me as far as the young ladies were concerned. Not only had my confidence increased, I had shot up and the fat had dropped off me to be replaced by muscle. My sexual activity began when I was about 15 when I met a lovely girl, half-Indian she was, but after that there'd been a bit of a drought in that department until I started working the doors.

I digress. I wasn't so much a bouncer – more a hard line negotiator. I'd be the one, when all else failed, who had to step in. Trouble is, in that game, people don't always want to talk, especially when they've got a bit of booze or coke in them. That's when they all think they can beat each other up. That's the worst thing. Drink and drugs change normal people into what they think is someone like Superman. Sometimes, normally nice guys get a bit of beer in them and begin behaving like idiots. They start believing they can fight and want one. They are so sure they can do it. Until they wake up with a big black eye and a busted jaw.

I remember an incident that occurred soon after I began working on the doors. I got nicked in the stomach by some little git with a Stanley knife but I didn't even feel it. It must have been due to the adrenaline rush at the time.

Around the same time, I lost a good colleague, Dave Anderson. He was killed at Bagley's nightclub in Islington when he was stabbed in the back. I heard there had been some aggravation in the club with a drug dealer. Dave had chucked him out, but the guy came back inside, got behind Dave, and stabbed him.

Dave was a consummate professional doorman. He only weighed around 11 stone but he had one of the best left hooks I've ever seen. If ever he had the hump, you'd see it in his eyes and, frankly, that could scare the life out of you.

It's ironic, I can remember Dave telling me that it wouldn't take a hard man to stab you in the back. Sadly, those words were prophetic. I can also remember Dave telling me how, when we were both working at The Venue, a guy had come up to him and said that the geezer working upstairs that night (me) didn't look up to much. Dave had asked him who he meant.

'That geezer with the glasses,' he replied.

'Oh yeah,' said Dave, 'Why don't you go upstairs and tell him that to his face – he'll knock you spark out!'

Dave always reckoned that, if a doorman didn't look the part, he'd only be doing the job for one of two reasons – he's either a fuckin' nutter – or he can really look after himself.

I reckon Dave must have been in his mid-30s when he was killed. His death brought it home to us that just one bad night could have ruined it for any of us, and we often had people either trying to attack or threaten us with knives. In fact, we had plenty of that while we were working at The Venue, especially in the first few months when we really had to earn our money.

It was particularly hard work there at times. Even though there were thick metal doors, we'd still get people trying to smash their way through them. People used to come from the pub across the road dressed in shirts and jeans which didn't conform to the dress code at The

Venue. Our shift – me, Matty Austin Cooper, Johnny Fast Hands, John Novo, Terry O'Neill and Simon Andrews – were kept pretty busy with the likes of them.

But door work isn't all about fighting. I'm 36 now and have been doing this sort of work for years, but there's only been about 15 occasions when I've had to get my hands dirty. I've been known to get into more trouble when I've been going out on my own.

It was while I was working at The Venue that I got involved in a bare-knuckle fight. A karate expert, who used to hang around the area, had thrown out a challenge. He wanted to know if anyone was game enough to take him on outside. There were plenty of bodybuilder types who frequented the club but none of them were up for it. I was, though. The curly-haired kid from Woodford relished the opportunity to prove himself.

It was around 2.30am My shift had just finished so I wandered around to the back of the premises. The karate geezer was there limbering up and a sizeable crowd had gathered, waiting to see what would happen.

'Is this the geezer I'm fighting?' he said when I appeared.

'Yeah'.

He held out his hand to shake at just the moment my left hook knocked him spark out. I wasn't there to muck about. So there it was, my one and only bare-knuckle fight ended after just one punch and I hadn't been touched.

That's my style, see. I don't want to get hurt so, if I

see even the slightest opportunity to put someone out of the game before they can get at me, I'll take it every time.

When the bands had finished playing at The Venue it was often our job to ensure no-one climbed up onto the empty stage, which is always a temptation for those who fancy showing off a bit. One night, as it was getting pretty late, a few punters were trying to climb onto the stage. I was already on it and was pushing them back, but one of them was pretty persistent. Time and again he tried, and it soon became obvious he was pissed out of his head. I repeatedly asked him to stop messing about, but he wouldn't listen so, with my foot, I pushed him backwards. As he fell, he disappeared from my view, but my colleagues picked him up and took him outside. The following evening he returned. Sober this time, he asked me if he had behaved the previous night.

'Yeah, why?' I replied.

He grinned widely at me to reveal a gap where his two front teeth had been.

'How did that happen then?'

'Some big lump pushed me off the stage last night!'

When I was about 19, I went to visit Freddy at his home on the Broadmead Estate. Freddy lived on the ninth floor so I got into the lift and found myself face to face with the black kid who had beaten me up so badly when I was 11.

By now, of course, I looked considerably different.

I'd shot up and had developed a good physique as a result of regular workouts in the gym. On top of that I'd been working doors so I was pretty confident – I just knew I could bang people out.

I looked right at the black kid and it was obvious he didn't recognise me.

'Hello mate, you okay?' I said.

'Good,' he said, 'what floor?'

'Eleven.'

He pressed the button for the 11th floor, then looked right at me and said, 'Do I know you?'

I said, 'Don't you remember?' and then WHAM! I knocked him spark out on the floor and gave him a kicking for good measure.

The doors opened at the 11th floor. I exited the lift and walked down two flights of stairs to Freddy's. I never said a word to anyone about what happened that day, but it didn't take long for word to get around.

The worm had turned.

Chapter Four

HIRED MUSCLE

I've often been in bars and clubs and had fights with people I don't really know. My life had got so mad. My mate The Tall Fella, me and a few others would always stick together and would go everywhere. We were known at a popular nightclub in Gants Hill. We never had to pay for anything. We'd just bowl up and it felt like we owned the place. We'd be there every Thursday, Friday, Saturday and Sunday and, each night, someone would get knocked out. That's how it was.

Johnny Fast Hands always used to say 'even if you're wrong, you're right'. That's how we were. If one of us got into a ruck, even if we'd got it wrong, we'd still help each other out. Afterwards, we'd say 'what was that all about?' It was such a bullshit world where you couldn't be seen to be losing face. It's a load of crap, and all it does is get you into a load of trouble. Bottom line, it got me a really bad name but, when you're working the doors, you really can't afford to appear divided in front of the punters. Unity is strength.

Over the years us doormen have stuck together through thick and thin and, between us, we've all had to help each other out from time to time. One night, Johnny Fast Hands and me were outside a bar by the taxi rank when we became aware of a geezer giving the owner of the bar a hard time. I went over to tell the geezer to shut up and to get into the waiting taxi where his mate and two birds were already sitting in the back seat. The geezer reluctantly opened the taxi door and sat in the front passenger seat. 'Do us a favour,' I said to the taxi driver, 'just take him away.' Meanwhile, as I had been watching the geezer in the front, without me noticing, the guy who had been sitting in the back of the taxi had got out and was walking around the taxi towards me.

Suddenly, I heard Johnny yell out, 'Look out Dom!' but, before I could react I was aware of BANG, BANG, BANG, BANG, four punches in rapid succession as Johnny hit him before he could land one on me. A friend of mine, Alan the Hairdresser, could hardly believe his eyes. 'Fuckin' 'ell Dom, did you see that?'

I hadn't. That's because the geezer we'd just shoved into the front of the taxi had decided he fancied having a go too and was about to try to climb out of the taxi. The window was open so I just landed one on his chin and he went flying back down into his seat. I'd knocked him out cold. The taxi driver, however, wasn't so impressed.

'I'm not likely to get a tip off him now, am I? I guess I'll have to wake him up first!'

Mind you, he was impressed with Johnny. 'Fuck me, your mate's got fast hands – and can't he hit!'

Hence the nickname, Johnny Fast Hands.

Johnny's a good old boy, that's for sure. Mind you, if ever you get the hump with him, you just want to kill him but, after ten minutes or so, he'll have you laughing your head off. But it's on the door or in tight situations he really comes into his own. He would never leave your side, no matter what. In fact, if ever someone would even suggest he lacked bottle, I reckon he'd go straight out and do something really stupid just to prove them wrong.

Big John is of a similar ilk. He's as game as you like. He never backs away from anything, which is why he's got as many lumps and bumps as the rest of us. He's an old school doorman. He'll tell you to fuck off and, if you don't like it, he'll offer you a back-hander, but at least you know where you stand with someone like him.

That's not to say Big John goes out looking for aggro, although once he paid a heavy price for pushing his luck a little too far. It was Christmas Eve when Big John upset some people he shouldn't have in a pub and ended up with having his throat cut. That's the way it is in these circles. As I found out myself, if you upset the wrong people, you have to expect to pay the price.

I reckon, at the end of the day, Big John got lucky. It's not often someone gets their throat slit with a blade and still lives to tell the tale but, fortunately, his injuries didn't turn out to be life-threatening because he received the appropriate treatment in good time. Nevertheless, he had around ten stitches put in to seal the wound.

But, if Big John had had his own way, he wouldn't even have been taken to hospital in the first place. He didn't want to be seen to be making a fuss about it, but the ambulance crew who were called out to the incident practically insisted they should take him straight to the hospital.

I suppose you could defend Big John in that he was pissed out of his skull when the incident occurred but, as he'd upset the wrong guys, they served him up. Simple as that.

Like Big John, his attackers were all boxing fans and they had often come along to watch me box. It turned out that the guy who actually cut Big John was a friend of mine which, in a way, was a godsend because, later, I was able to encourage all involved in the incident to get together for a big pow-wow in order to sort things out.

They spoke about what happened that day. It turned out that my mate had been going through a transitional stage in his life known as The 12 Steps, part of an Alpha Christian course which preaches the power of forgiveness. If you've ever hurt someone in the past, you should find them and apologise for what you've done. As a result, he apologised to Big John for cutting him. For his part, Big John admitted he had been out of order too. 'I called it on, but came off second best.' At the end of the day, the guys are never going to be the best of friends but at least they can now all sit down together and have a cup of coffee.

Further on in this book you'll read about some more of the troubles I've experienced. In spite of all the risks at those times, Big John was prepared to lay his life on the line in order to stand by me when I really needed him. That meant such a lot to me. He may have a bit of a belly on him these days, but he can still have a bit of a tear-up, no question about that. If Big John hits you with his right hand, it's goodnight!

Top Guard was a reputable company and provided plenty of opportunities for work. Nowadays, Big John, a few others and me regularly work the doors at nightclubs and pubs. We also do quite a bit of event security, such as boxing promotions for the likes of Frank Warren and Barry Hearn. We do security work at music concerts at London Arena, Wembley, and the Brixton Academy amongst others. That's probably where I got my love of music as, in the past, I've got to see some really obscure bands that have since gone on to become really well known.

Looking back, there have been a number of times when I've had to get my hands dirty in my line of work. There are often confrontations and, if you're not sure you can handle yourself, believe me, this is not the job for you. Of course, you have to try to calm down situations before they get out of hand but, sometimes, that just isn't possible. Sometimes, a bit of force is all some people understand.

To be honest, I can't really say that in the past when the fists started flying I always expected to come out on top. It wasn't a consideration. When I lost my rag I just blanked everything out and, once I let the first punch go, I was away. I've always been a durable sort of fella inside and outside of a boxing ring. Maybe it was even a fear thing – I never wanted to get hurt. That's why I always got it over and done with as fast as I could.

Have I ever come off worst? Only once, if you count the gym attack but, even then, I reckon I could claim a draw. I suppose I've been very lucky. Whenever I'm in a tight spot I react straight away and worry about the consequences later because, at the end of the day, I don't want anyone to hurt me. I'd rather hurt them. When you box, everything you do is premeditated. The nerves build up but, if I found myself in an altercation suddenly outside the doors of a nightclub, it would be bang, bang, bang, all over. There'd be no time for nerves.

I was usually quite mellow when I worked the doors. I never tried to instigate a situation because I knew that if I banged some geezer out I'd then have the job of waking him up and then I'd still have the hassle of getting rid of him.

Big John and me used to work outside a well-known nightclub in Kentish Town. We used to work the queue for a bit of extra cash. Basically, those waiting to come into the club had to line up between zig-zag barriers.

Big John and me would walk up and down the line and, if we saw someone who wasn't fitting in with the club's strict dress code – clubbers had to wear smart casual clothes – no jeans or trainers – we'd have to tell them, 'Sorry mate, not tonight.'

One night, it was bitterly cold, we were walking the line when five guys turned up, giving it large. They joined the queue. One of them looked right at me. 'You alright mate, what are you looking at?' He didn't realise I was working for the club. All the security staff at the club wore T-shirts with SECURITY printed on them but, as we were outside, we'd been wearing coats over our shirts to keep warm. The guy and his mates continued being a bit lippy so I went up to the guy working the door and told him, 'Don't let that lot in.' The guys began laughing at me but their smiles soon vanished when I told them I was a member of the security staff.

'You've just taken part in an aptitude test boys,' I said, 'But you've failed miserably!'

I got hold of the really lippy one and dragged him around the corner to teach him a lesson in manners. 'Please don't hit me, please don't hit me,' he was squealing. Big John tapped me on the shoulder to remind me there was a CCTV camera overhead.

'You cheeky bugger,' I said to the wimp. 'Fuck off.' He'd had a lucky let-off.

One incident at this nightclub left a particularly nasty taste in my mouth. I was working the doors when, suddenly, there was a punch-up in the foyer which began to get right out of hand. When I intervened, one of the guys in the punch-up turned on me so I hit him and laid him out. As I did so, a couple of others grabbed me and we all ended up on the floor. Almost immediately, someone was stamping down on my head while someone else was kicking me.

With my arms pinned to my side and with this guy's face pushed right against mine, there were very few options open to me. I was getting badly hurt and I know that desperate times call for desperate measures. I managed to turn my head to one side, and then survival mode kicked in. I opened my mouth and bit down hard on his cheek in an attempt to make him let go. But he didn't, at least not until a chunk of his flesh came away into my mouth. It was really, really gross – and by that, I mean for me!

The guy was screaming and screaming in absolute agony. I jumped upright as soon as I got the opportunity. My face was badly swollen from the attack and I was really shaken up. I looked down at the guy and saw the blood pissing out of the side of his face as his mate, who I'd earlier knocked over, picked him up and they ran off down the road. As they disappeared, I spat out a bloody lump of flesh.

Altercations, though, sometimes had a more amusing side. I remember working in a nightclub with an old friend, Charlie Thompson, when a fight broke out on the dance floor. One of the women who worked at the club came running up to us. 'Dom, Charlie, come quickly.' Personally, I couldn't really see why we were needed as there were already plenty of security staff at the scene. Nevertheless, I got one of the fellas involved in the fight in a necklock while Charlie got hold of his legs, and we carried him out.

Afterwards, Charlie and me were standing in the foyer having a chat with the other security staff. 'What were you thinking of?' I asked them. 'There were five of you there and between you, you couldn't get one guy out?' While we were talking Charlie was standing with his back to the door. Out of the corner of my eye I noticed the fella we had just chucked out was re-entering the club, holding his shoe aloft and was about to bring it down onto the back of Charlie's head.

'Chaaarlie!'

Too late… 'Ouch!'

Unfortunately for the fella, Charlie had been a very good amateur boxer so you can probably imagine what happened next.

Charlie and I have often worked together, either on security at boxing bills, or on the doors or doing security work. He's typical of most of my colleagues in that he'll never leave your side in a ruck, no matter what.

One night Charlie and I were working together in a nightclub when a girl and her boyfriend began arguing drunkenly with each other. It looked as if they were about to come to blows so Charlie and I went over to break it up. Suddenly she turned on us. 'Look out Charlie!' I shouted but, again, I was too late, as she raked her fingernails down the side of his face, inflicting deep scratch marks that bled profusely.

I pushed her away from Charlie but, in doing so, I

made her stumble and she fell backwards onto the floor and she was temporarily knocked out. Now, let's make one thing clear – I don't hit women. This was a complete accident. Had she been sober, I'm sure she wouldn't have fallen over at all. While all this was going on, her boyfriend was ejected from the club. Moments later, the girl came around and she was also ejected. However, it seems, the girl telephoned the police and, before long, they arrived and promptly nicked a big Somalian doorman who we called Tikkamala. Quite why they arrested him we weren't sure.

Then the girl telephoned her parents. They soon turned up and it was obvious her father was spoiling for a fight: 'Look what one of your doormen's done to my daughter!' For once I found myself actually trying to calm down a situation. I tried to explain to the father how drunk his daughter and her boyfriend had been and what had happened to Charlie's face. To prove my point, I called Charlie over so the father could see, first hand, what his daughter had done.

That did it. Suddenly, he went potty, grabbed his daughter and bundled her into his car, only waiting to tell her boyfriend to fuck off before driving away. At this point, the Old Bill let Tikkamala go. To our surprise, a week later, the father returned to the club to apologise for his daughter's actions. We actually ended up having a beer with him.

These days my colleagues Big John, Paul Biggs, Big Dave Ferris, and Kev Webster and me often provide security cover on a sub-contract basis for Ian McAllister who owns M.A.N. Commercial Security, one of the biggest companies of its kind in Britain.

Big Dave and Kev won't back down to anyone. They're great blokes and I think we all work well together. Perhaps you meet certain people for a reason. With Dave, although it can be weeks between meeting up with each other, we're very close. A family man, Dave's in his 40s. He's a big man, taller than me, and he's a black belt in karate. He's fit too. He trains all the time.

Kev's a black-belt judo expert who's represented Britain. If you look at Big Dave and Kev together, I guess they look just like who they are. When we work together, Paul and Johnny Fast Hands are usually the negotiators, while Big Dave, Kev and me are the muscle who, if required, do what we have to do.

M.A.N. provides all kinds of security cover, from personal to site security, anything in fact. I've known the company owner Ian since I was 19. I first met him at a boxing bill at York Hall, Bethnal Green, when I was working for Top Guard. Ian used to bring his men down from Birmingham if there was a big show.

Sometimes, through Ian, we find ourselves providing security at the ExCel Centre in London's Docklands at boxing evenings. It's a huge place and we use up to ten supervisors because it's such a big job. Usually, me, Paul, Dave and Big John will supervise the whole event, while another guy, Steve Tysall, runs the ringside area security.

Recently, at a boxing bill, a guy was getting in people's way by standing up in front of them as they tried to watch the contests. One of the security men working alongside me had a quiet word with him and asked him to sit down, but he refused.

Enter Dominic Negus.

I grabbed him by the arm and said, 'If you don't fuckin' move, I'll sling you outside and you can watch it on the telly later!' That's what I'm there for. The geezer wasn't taking any notice, so what was the point of being nice to him?

We get a lot of work through Ian, particularly in the London area. I remember when we used to provide security cover in television studios, including the Frank Skinner and David Baddiel programme. On one of the shows, Baddiel spotted me standing next to another bald guy and began taking the piss out of us. He reckoned we looked like a pair of tits!

Another guy, Steve, who worked for Top Guard, went on to open his own company and did pretty well for himself. Me, Paul Biggs and Big John spent some time working for him, in my case, just to top up my earnings from my freelance work. I was grateful for the work Steve put my way – and there was plenty of it as he had a contract with a top boxing promoter.

That line of work saw Paul Biggs and me working in Manchester to prepare the security arrangements for a boxing bill at the MEN Arena. We travelled north on the Friday and arrived in time to help supervise the weigh-in. After that we had the evening to ourselves.

We had a few drinks with the guys from the British Boxing Board of Control, then went to bed.

Early next morning, Paul had found the gym in the hotel and had gone in for a workout. I decided to have a look around outside. It was around 8.30am. I walked along the road from the hotel and spotted a McDonald's restaurant that was open and decided to pop in to grab a bite to eat.

Standing near the counter were three scruffy-looking geezers amongst a few other people. In fact, the three scruffs were just what they looked like. It was obvious they were crackheads. They each had three cups of coffee and around 40 sachets of sugar. When I went in, they stopped talking and looked straight at me. 'Got any change mate?' said one of them to me. I should have kept my mouth shut but replied, 'No mate, I haven't got any.'

They recognised from my accent that I wasn't from around those parts. 'Come on, you soft southerner.'

'Look mate, don't start.' After that, I just ignored them and ordered my breakfast. Then one of them came right up to me, real close. I told him to stand back because I wasn't going to give him anything. By now his chest was against my hand. As far as I was concerned, he was in my space and for all I knew, he might be just about to jab me with some dirty needle. There was no way I was going to risk it. No way I was prepared to give him a second chance, so I just pinged him with a right hander and he went over.

Then one of his mates fancied a go so I did him with

a left hook and he was sitting on his arse on top of a table. The other crackhead just stood there not knowing what to do.

'I'm sorry about that,' I said to the girl who had been serving me.

'Oh, that's okay,' she replied, 'they're just a bloody nuisance.'

By the time I got back to the hotel, Paul had been wondering where I'd been. 'I've just had a punch-up in McDonald's,' I told him.

'You bugger, Dom,' he said. 'I just can't take you anywhere!'

Steve also found us work at the London Eye, a popular tourist attraction on the Embankment in the capital. This was a brilliant job. Big John and I had to patrol the Embankment to the Royal Festival Hall in order to ensure there were no illegal traders setting up, that nobody took photographs in restricted areas, and that no television camera crews were working in the area without the appropriate permits. But although the work was fine, the money was crap. I once worked a whole month – 11 hour days – and still didn't have enough money to cover my rent.

Thank goodness for the boxing security contract. Trouble was, Steve fell out with the promoter and, suddenly, the boxing work dried up. The promoter telephoned Paul Biggs and asked if he would like to run the security operation instead. He agreed and contacted me to see if I would come on board. I dithered a while because, although the income from Steve was paltry, it was pretty regular and I didn't want to jump ship if Paul couldn't provide regular work. But Paul could offer me double the wages Steve was offering and I had bills to pay. I agreed to join Paul.

We knew this could cause friction and, not surprisingly, Paul and Steve fell out big time. Paul had been practically a right-hand man to Steve but, since the boxing contract had ended, Paul too had been struggling financially. By cutting out Steve, we'd be doing the same work as before, but without the middle man.

I've known Paul for a few years now. He's really got the gift of the gab. He's great for the security work we do and, if he can't calm down a incident by having a quiet word, the chances are we'll be having a bad situation. You just know it's going to kick off. If Paul tells someone off, it's like listening to a teacher scolding a kid. He's nice, but firm. He's a good front man to have alongside you because he's so good at defusing situations before they get out of hand.

I really enjoy working alongside Paul but, when Steve began to bad mouth him at every opportunity, it really niggled me. I called into Steve's office to have a word. I wanted to tell him he should be quiet and leave it alone. That way we could just forget it and move on. After all, the boxing work had dried up because of his disagreement with the boxing promoter. It had had nothing to do with Paul.

But Steve wasn't there so I left a message. A few days later, Steve telephoned me. He was convinced the boxing promoter or one of his associates had sent me round to his office to beat him up and it took me ages to convince him otherwise.

My involvement in some rather shady business arrangements came about through working the doors. At this point I should mention that anything I did that was less than above board had nothing to do with Top Guard, which is a reputable company.

People would often come up to me to relate their problems. Maybe they were publicans with an in-house problem that required a bit of muscle and, it seems, there were plenty of naughty pubs around. Usually around six of us would go into a problem pub. We'd buy drinks then three of us would sit in one corner, three in the other and we'd just watch to see what developed. Usually we'd been brought in because of persistent troublemakers. Sometimes it was drug dealers. Either way, it didn't really matter that much to us. At the end of the day it was just another job.

We'd just bash 'em up in front of everyone or, sometimes, we'd wait for them to go into the toilet and follow them in. Me, I was always there to teach people a lesson. I was pretty considerate though because I always told them exactly why I'd bashed them and then say something along the lines of, 'We don't want scum like you in here, get out!'

But they always *had* to be bashed. Talk's cheap you see and actions speak louder than words. 'This is what you get if you come back – this was just a taster.'

We did a lot of that sort of work, plus I made a little extra cash by collecting dodgy debts. At one time I did legitimate collections with all the correct paperwork and everything. But that soon changed. Who did I collect for? Sometimes I had no idea. Often I would be approached by intermediaries who would come to me and say this much money is owed to so and so. Can you get it off A but don't give it to B – give it to C. The debt work has seen me turn up at a lot of people's doorsteps, but I had one rule that I always stuck to – I'd never collect cash for drugs or porn clients.

There were debts for all sorts – deals involving alcohol and fags and several involving motors. It wasn't uncommon to hear of someone acquiring a 30 grand motor and only paying up a grand. These were routine jobs for us but we usually came through okay in the end. At first we used to come down quite hard on debtors but, after a while, we began to realise it wasn't always necessary to do so. We'd start off by asking them if they were the people responsible for the debt. When, eventually, we got that out of them, we'd start negotiating with them. Sometimes, even if at first we'd got a bit heavy with them, we'd end up sorting it all out over a cup of tea!

I've collected arrears for legitimate car dealers or car hire firms with the proper paperwork on a number of occasions. Often, vehicles would be hired but not returned, or maybe someone had the use of a company vehicle and didn't seem to be in too much of a hurry to return it. Then I'd turn up with a colleague and a low loader to take it back.

Alcohol and cigarette deals are probably two of the

biggest earners out there. If someone had acquired a delivery of booze or cigarettes on behalf of someone who was too slow to pay up for them, people would be employed to hurry things along. It wasn't uncommon for sums of up to £20,000 to be outstanding.

Occasionally I found myself collecting unpaid cash for building work. Perhaps people were not wanting or able to pay for work done. I think I was always fair though. Usually, if I could see there was no way someone could pay up for whatever reason, I didn't get too heavy with them. After all, you can't get blood out of a stone.

On the other hand, some people have short arms and deep pockets. I remember once going to collect some money on behalf of a builder from a guy who'd had a 15 grand brick wall built around his house in Luton. I turned up on his doorstep and he got clever.

'What do you reckon you're gonna do if I said I won't pay for it?' he said.

'Not a lot,' I replied.

'Fuck off then, you're not getting any money off me.'

I said okay and walked away. The geezer laughed and shut his door. A couple of minutes later, when he looked out of his window, he saw I'd already smashed down a fair bit of his wall with a sledgehammer. It might have been a dead debt but, in this business, it's swings and roundabouts.

Like I mentioned earlier, it's the fear of violence that can often be more frightening than the violence itself. Sometimes it's just enough for people to know that you know where they live. Things like that can really get to people. Probably, though, in only maybe one out of ten cases, have we ever really had to get heavy to recover a debt. Johnny Fast Hands and me have done a lot of debt work together. It's just a job. Johnny was very good at talking to people. I was there more as a presence.

Once we found ourselves visiting a hairdressing salon in Stratford, east London. The guy who owned the salon owed money for some building work. We popped in and asked for him. He wasn't there so Johnny even left his phone number! We left a message that our visit was regarding a sum of money owed and we needed to speak to him. The next day Johnny was sitting on the bog when his phone rang.

'You came into my salon yesterday asking for money.'

'Yeah. Do you know X?'

'This ain't his debt is it?'

'Yeah.'

'Oh shit!'

In the end, he paid me and Johnny to leave it. 'I'll sort it out with X myself,' he said and gave us a grand each to let it go. We've had quite a few like that over the years. But, at the end of the day, there are no free lunches in this world. I guess we had a 90 per cent success rate collecting debts. We've even had occasions when, by the time we arrived, the money had already been paid. Seems we'd just been sent along to keep them on their toes. This was at a time when I would have knocked on my neighbour's door for a debt because I needed the money. Later on though, I was able to pick and choose which jobs I went on. Another tactic we used was to make out it was *our* money that was owed. That usually geed them up a bit.

I had a shock one day. I went to a house to collect a debt. A little boy was standing by the gate. His father started crying when he saw me. 'What are you crying about?' I asked. 'Please, please, don't take my son away!' I couldn't believe it. 'What do you think I am?' I said. 'I'm not an animal. I've just come to see if you can pay some of the money back.'

On occasions though, we've had people just come flying out at us. When that happens, well, you've just got to do what you've got to do. But it was only on rare occasions when I had to get my hands dirty. In one out of, say, every ten collections I might have had to give a little slap, one out of 20, a bit of a dig but, once they'd admitted they were the person who owed the money, we'd get them on the phone to whoever we were working for so they also knew we'd done our job.

I haven't worked for Top Guard for some years now. These days, Paul Biggs, Big Dave and Kev and me are self-employed as far as the security work is concerned, working on a sort of mercenary basis if you like. Word of mouth is how we get most of our work and, if you're any good at it, there's plenty of work out there.

We've worked with all sorts of people, some well-known, some not. We've worked with money or car dealers or people just doing business who feel safer to have the back-up of a minder close to hand. I've done plenty of driver-minder work for business people who have fallen out with their associates. I've taken many of them to meetings and they seem much more reassured to know they have the back-up of a bit of muscle.

German supermodel Claudia Schiffer was one of our clients, a really nice lady. We were assigned to look after her for a couple of days while she attended the car show at Earls Court in London. Basically, we just took her to and fro. We didn't actually speak to her that much, although she seemed to appreciate a few of my dirty jokes! She wouldn't remember me, I'm sure but, all the same, it was a privilege to work with her. She always had a lovely smile for everybody.

At the time she was seeing Tim Jeffries, the Green Shield Stamps heir, who turned out to be a real gent. There were three of us working on this job. We had to pick her up from his flat. I shared the first car with Claudia, while the others were in a car close behind.

Whenever we got back to Tim's flat we were invited in for a cuppa, which was really nice of them, but we said no thanks because, as far as we were concerned, that would have been crossing the line professionally.

There are many aspects to providing security at boxing shows. One of them is escorting the boxers from their dressing room to the ring and back again. That's not such a bad job. Sometimes you might get an irate fan, but usually they do little more than shout out abuse, especially if they've been drinking.

Normally, I don't find I have too much to do other than pushing people back to clear the way for the boxer I'm escorting. Of course, there are occasions when you may have to give someone a bit of a slap to calm them down but, when all's said and done, it's a lot less hassle than working the doors, that's for sure. And, of course, when I'm working at the boxing shows I'm pretty well known in those circles so people don't tend to take so many liberties when they see me.

I remember the time I escorted former world middleweight champion Chris Eubank to the ring. He's a really great bloke. I actually got to know Chris a bit after I became a professional boxer, although I have to admit, I don't know him well. Of course he's a bit eccentric, but it's not put on, that's the way he really is. The bottom line though is that man really knew how to box. He was brilliant. Who could ever forget his clash with Nigel Benn? In fact, as much as I love Benn, I reckon Chris was the better boxer of the two, yet I still reckon he was under-rated. I know some people reckon he's rude, but he was always fine with me.

Recently, we were doing the security work for the UB40 tour. We started at The Marquee at Wembley and then, for the last three days, at the National Exhibition Centre in Birmingham. They were really nice fellas, really professional. Working with them so often was a privilege, especially as we got to hear their music, though I have to say, when you've heard the same show every night, it does take the shine off it.

The work usually involves escorting the band from their tour bus, through the crowds to their dressing room. When we get the cue, we then escort them to the stage and stand next to it while they perform just in case the odd idiot wants to jump up on stage to join them. We make sure the bands are okay and, once they're done, we take them back to the dressing room and wait outside while, often, there's a VIP party backstage. Once we've got them back safely to their bus or limousine they go home and so do we. That's the nicer side of the work.

Often we are assigned as a pit team, working as a barrier between the fans and the stage. If we're on close security – that's actually on stage with the band – the pit crew are usually able to ensure that anyone attempting to jump right across the pit onto the stage are caught before they can do so. Occasionally, though, some people do get through, but they won't ever get past us – although sometimes the growing trend of crowd-surfing can cause a few problems for us security-wise.

I remember working at a concert by The Farm at the Astoria. As the band began singing their big hit 'Altogether Now', there was a sudden surge of fans, all steaming towards the stage. That night, we had our work cut out and had to be just a little more heavy-handed than this sort of work usually requires. Usually though, it's just good-natured over-enthusiasm from fans who have no intention of harming anyone. They just want to get that bit nearer their heroes.

We've worked for some brilliant bands and artists, including George Michael, U2, Carter USM and Richard Ashcroft (my favourite) at places like Earls

Court and Wembley Arena or smaller venues such as the Astoria in London's Charing Cross Road, and the Brixton Academy.

Mind you, some people we're paid to mind do have delusions of grandeur. I even wonder sometimes who it is I'm minding. I remember having to travel to an airport to be on hand to escort Simon Tong, the guitarist and keyboard player from the indie rock group The Verve, through the crowds to his limousine. As he came through arrivals he saw me and pushed his luggage trolley in my direction, expecting me to roll with it.

'Who do you think I am,' I said, 'Your bloody bag pusher?'

I told him I was there to look after him but I couldn't do much if someone had a pop at him if my hands were full while pushing his bloody bags around.

There's no shortage of work if you've got muscles and are prepared to use them to good effect. So it's not just debt collecting and minding jobs that came our way. Sometimes we'd be asked to help out at evictions. When we first started out we got a considerable amount of this kind of work. Johnny Fast Hands and me, together with a guy known only as The Captain, found ourselves in north east London on the behest of a guy who had bought a property to be redeveloped but the builders couldn't get in because a bunch of illegal asylum seekers had moved into it.

It had once been a beautiful old house, Victorian I reckon. It was one of a row of derelict houses of a good size but, because the builders had been unable to gain access, the bill was clocking up for the owner so time was of the essence.

When we arrived we knocked on the door which was answered by some young bird. We burst in past her. The Captain ran upstairs and, within moments we could hear him crashing around. I found a couple of geezers downstairs and told them to get their gear together and to fuck off. Then I made my way into one of the bedrooms where I was met by another geezer who had been watching television. He jumped up as I entered the room and pulled a carving knife on me but, before he could even think about what to do with it I laid him out with a right hook.

I went back downstairs and The Captain joined me. He was carrying a sledgehammer. Just to make his point and to show we meant business, he swung it right through a state-of-the-art widescreen telly!

Upstairs, the geezer I'd decked was beginning to come round. I found a suitcase, bunged a load of his stuff in it and chucked it through the window onto the street where it burst open, scattering his clothes everywhere.

All told, we chucked six geezers out of the premises and, at the very moment they left, the builders moved straight in and began changing the locks and securing the windows to stop them or anyone else getting in. Meanwhile, the asylum seekers promptly broke into the house next door and moved in there instead!

On another occasion, Johnny Fast Hands and me were asked to remove some student squatters from a house in north London. We travelled to the house accompanied by its owner, a property developer. Again, builders were outside, waiting to gain access so they could commence their work.

At the time I was having a lot of problems with my back and, as a result, it took quite a while to sledge-hammer our way through what proved to be a very tough front door.

Johnny was first through. We were greeted by some really loud music. Johnny looked through one of the doors. 'Here, Dom, look at this!' Inside the room, totally unaware of our presence, were two stark naked lesbians going at it for all they were worth. Their radio was so loud they hadn't even heard us! Mind you, they went bloody mad when they saw us and began calling us every name under the sun. We just told them to shut up, get dressed, and get out.

We made our way up the stairs. Behind a door we could hear a guy who sounded like he was French. He wouldn't open up and kept calling out, 'I've just come out of hospital!' I crashed against the door and it flew open, sending the Frenchman flying after it whacked him on the head. But it was an accident.

Meanwhile, it seems one of the students had managed to get to a phone to call the Old Bill. Hearing them pull up outside the house I realised I had to think fast. Spotting a bucket in one of the rooms, I picked it up and the sledgehammer in my other hand.

As I strolled down the stairs I was met by coppers running up them.

'What's going on?' said one of them.

'Dunno mate, we're just the workers. Better ask one of them up there.'

The coppers made their way to the top floor. Meanwhile, Johnny and I legged it before the coppers realised they'd been hoodwinked.

Nevertheless, their intervention meant we hadn't fully succeeded in clearing the house. We already had a telephone number for the guy who had been described to us as the main squatter and it didn't take us long to find out where he was. He wasn't a dropout. He had a good job, with regular money coming in. It's just that he believed in squatters' rights.

We spotted him sitting in a coffee shop, parked up outside and rang his number. He picked up his phone. 'We know where you live, and we know where you work. Why don't you look out the window?'

Moments later, he called back. 'Listen, can you give me a week? After that, we'll be out.' They kept their word but, if we hadn't threatened them with violence, I really don't think it would have worked because he knew his legal rights.

One day, a friend called me wanting to pick my brains about something. We hadn't seen each other for some time, but we agreed to meet up for a coffee. He asked me if I remembered a kitchen fitter who had been doing work at his house. Apparently, the fitter had persuaded my mate to invest some money in his company but he later claimed things had gone a bit pear-shaped so he wasn't able to give my mate back his cash. To make matters worse, he'd told my mate that *I* was helping him sort out his finances.

That was a lie.

The fitter was using me as a bumper in the hope my mate wouldn't get too heavy on him when he wanted his money back. Fortunately though, my mate quickly realised what the fitter was trying to do.

I suggested we should set up a meeting with the fitter the next day, somewhere not too out of the way, somewhere he'd feel safe. We decided on the local coffee shop. My mate arrived first of all, and then along came the fella who, we knew, had a penchant for telling porkies. He'd been going around telling anyone who'd listen he'd been in the SAS and that he'd been fighting in the Gulf War, but we knew that was a load of bollocks.

Believe me, I know a few guys in the armed forces and I take my hat off to them all. They are the real hard men, guys risking their lives while we all sleep safely in our beds. Anyway, this particular fella reckoned he'd been captured and tortured, God knows what else. All his lies and his tale about me being involved in sorting out his finances didn't exactly endear him to me.

As soon as I arrived at the coffee shop and saw him the juices began to flow. There were butterflies in my stomach as I questioned myself about what I should do next. He was sitting at a table with my mate, exchanging pleasantries as I walked over to join them. However, at that very moment, an old friend spotted me so we had the quickest of chats before I sat down next to the others. My mate was obviously pleased to see me, but the kitchen fitter was really taken aback by my sudden arrival.

'Hello,' I said as I sat down and made myself welcome at their table.

The fitter told me it was great to see me but, if I didn't mind, he was having a meeting. 'I know,' I said, 'I arranged it.' You should have seen his face, it was like someone had just told him his cock had fallen off! He knew he'd been rumbled.

He tried making all sorts of excuses but, when he said he hadn't told my mate I'd been helping him out, my mate had a right go at him and asked him why he'd dropped my name into it in the first place.

After a few seconds of watching the fitter squirming uncomfortably in his seat I decided to put him out of his misery. I asked him how he intended to repay my mate. He told me he'd been trying to get a bank loan, but it was obvious he was bullshitting me. I told him he'd better pay up and be quick about it, and then the idiot decided to get a bit shirty with me.

Not a smart move.

I put my hands around his neck and gave a good squeeze. It might not be the flashest move in the book, but it usually gets the job done pretty quickly. I was telling him he had to pay my mate back his money by the weekend and, that for a guy who had supposedly served in the SAS, his face was a picture!

Then I pulled him up from his chair and nutted him.

He ended up sitting on the floor, dazed as you like, with a big lump appearing on his forehead. As he held his head in his hands I reminded him he had until the weekend to pay up. As he got up I gave him a left hook on the chin and sent him back to the floor with his legs in the air and the remains of two cups of coffee all over his clean, white shirt.

At this point I noticed an elderly couple who had been sitting at a nearby table. They'd been watching everything that had been going on. As I was leaving I went over to them, apologised for what had happened, and offered to pay for their coffees. The lady told me that the fella must have upset me a lot and must have deserved what he got. Her husband told me not to worry about it, in fact, it had brightened up his day; he thought things like that only happened in *EastEnders*!

It may have been an ugly incident, but at least it did the trick. By the weekend my mate had been repaid the money owed to him, and he treated me to a blinding drink for my help, so everyone was happy.

Except, of course, for the bloke with the lump on his head and coffee all over his shirt.

Chapter Five

KOSTYA TSZYU AND THE PRINCE

In June 2005, we were assigned to provide security for one of the boxers I admired most of all, Australian-Russian IBF world welterweight champion Kostya Tszyu who had come over to defend his title against Ricky Hatton at the MEN Arena in Manchester.

Boxing-wise, I was well aware of Kostya's abilities. I held him in very high regard, and I know Ricky Hatton did too. At that stage in his career Kostya was probably one of the best pound-for-pound boxers in the world, a consummate professional. Having said that, we didn't know quite what to expect of him as a person when we first met him and his large entourage, which included Glenn Jennings, one of the greatest boxing trainers in Australia.

Of course, in our line of work you need to know just

how far you should go should things go awry. As far as I'm concerned, it all depends on what the job is about. We have our boundaries. Me, I'll guard a person as if they're my best friend. It was like that with Kostya, one of the biggest jobs we've taken on – two weeks from when he landed at the airport to the day he left.

This assignment meant working until late at night and starting around 6am each morning because Kostya would usually want to go out running. We'd be in a van behind him and his running partners while, a bit further ahead, there would be another van with more minders. I wasn't in the van to drive it. My role was to be ready to jump out quickly just in case anyone tried it on. Kostya is so well-known in boxing circles but, on the streets around Bolton, no-one really seemed to realise who he was.

Even though, to be honest, we were hoping Ricky would win because we've often worked with him, we became very close to Kostya during the time we spent with him. We began by asking him exactly what he required of us. Would we let people up to him to sign autographs? Yes. So, whenever the crowds flocked to get his signature, the four of us would surround Kostya and let them through a few at a time. Good minders are usually just there to be seen as a deterrent.

My mum makes me laugh. She's often seen me on the telly while I'm doing the security work. When she heard I was working with Kostya she said, 'When you walk him out, wave!' I had to explain I couldn't. I'd be too busy doing my job.

Kostya would often ask for particular fruits, and he'd only drink certain milk, so we'd often have to go out in the van in search of his requirements prior to his 6am run. I say *have* to but that's not strictly accurate; once you've got close to someone like Kostya, you like to be able to give him that little bit extra.

As well as Glenn Jennings, working with Kostya gave me the opportunity to meet some really nice people, including a fella from Australia called Ronnie Nash who is a member of Kostya's management team, his wife Carrie, and Kostya's physician Dr Bill. They were accompanied by Johnny Lewis, the head of Kostya's training team. They were always with Kostya. However, after a short while, me and the lads were getting bad vibes and, to tell the truth, we were starting to get the hump over it. After all, we were trying to do our best for them all.

I said to Big Dave, Paul and Kev, 'this ain't right'. When we challenged Glenn and Johnny they admitted they had wondered if we might be spies from the Hatton camp, checking out Kostya's training methods and so on. Paul pulled Johnny to one side: 'I think we need to have a chat.'

'Of course we know Ricky,' I told him, 'But how long do you think we could work in this business if we were doing that sort of thing? People wouldn't touch us with a bargepole. That's why we get the work we do. If we fuck up with you, no-one else would want us.'

That seemed to smooth things out.

Everything Kostya and his team wanted, they got. This was the big league. A ring had been erected in the stadium in Bolton just for Kostya's use, and the punchbags were already set up. Kostya would be there from 3pm to 5pm each day. His sparring sessions were terrific. One of his sparring partners was Emmanuel Augustus who is well-known for lasting the distance and is himself a former IBF light welterweight Inter Continental champion who had already had huge battles against the likes of Floyd Mayweather Jnr, Leonardo Dorin and Jesus Sanchez, to name but a few.

Mayweather, a WBC champion, has actually admitted that the popular Augustus was probably the toughest opponent of his career, which just goes to show the calibre of sparring Kostya was getting the benefit of.

If I'm honest, after watching the way Kostya was moving around while sparring with Augustus, I really thought he had what it took to beat Ricky, even though Ricky also has a good team of people around him.

Prior to the fight, some other guys turned up, claiming they were also security for Kostya. 'Hold on,' I said, 'Where were you when he flew in?' One of them reckoned he ran a huge security business back in Australia, but I told him I didn't care what he did in Oz, while he was here in England he'd do exactly what we told him to.

We took Kostya to the arena to show him how we

were going to run the operation. The Aussie security guy had other ideas, but we insisted. In the end he agreed but, suddenly, Ronnie was getting a bit edgy.

Bearing in mind Kostya was a multi-million pound commodity we could understand his concerns, but I told him we would guarantee Kostya's safety because we were willing to do absolutely anything, whatever it would take, to ensure all went well on the night. That was good enough for Ronnie.

It proved to be a cracking fight. Although we'd wanted Ricky to win, we couldn't help feeling sad for Kostya when Ricky took his title. Kostya hadn't answered the bell for the 12th round, and was taken to hospital for a check-up. Dave and Paul went with him, although I couldn't help noticing that some of his own people didn't bother, and we were all waiting for him when he got back to his hotel at 6am the following morning so we could be sure he was alright.

Paul, Big Dave, Kev and me all laid down in the corridor outside his hotel room to grab some kip. Like I said, we never left Kostya for a moment, even when he was asleep and I can even remember Dr Bill coming out to take a photograph of us all outside Kostya's door. At around 11.30pm it opened again. Kostya appeared, still looking rather battered. He looked at us all and was almost in tears.

'I'm so sorry,' he said, 'I've let you all down.'

I replied, 'No mate, you'll always be a champion to me.'

It was a very emotional moment. Kostya realised we

did, indeed, really care about him and he was very appreciative. What a humble man.

It was the lull before the storm. The next day, Ricky turned up with his family. They'd come over to visit Kostya and his family who were already in the hotel with him. We took Ricky and his folks to the ballroom to meet them all. While they were all in there, loads of photographs were being taken. Kev was in the ballroom with them. I was outside the door. Suddenly Kev burst through. 'Fuckin' prick!'

It seems this bloke we called Aussie Dave, who was a member of Kostya's security team, had said something to upset him. Now Big Dave, Paul, Kev and me are all totally different characters. In some respects, I reckon they're more professional than me. If someone had upset me, I couldn't have walked out like Kev did. I'd have had it out with them there and then.

Once Kev had calmed down we all went back into the ballroom. They were still taking photographs. Kev went to one end of the room, Paul and Big Dave to the other, while I stood at the side. Then I heard, 'Oi boy, move.' It was Aussie Dave.

'Pardon?'

'Move out of the picture!'

I know the room was packed, but I went absolutely mad, right in front of them all.

'Who the fuckin' hell do you think you're talking to you little prick!'

'What?'

Above: Here I am, the curly-haired kid from Woodford with one of my first boxing trophies. I'm pictured with my trainer at Gator ABC, Gary Bedford.

Below: Me today, with a bit less hair on my head and a lot more fights, in and out of the ring, under my belt!

Above: Me and my Dad. If I could be half the father he was to my brother Freddy and me, I'll have it sussed. I miss him so much.

Below: My baby daughter Annabella and I pay my Mum a visit. I'm very close to my Mum. I guess I'll always be her little soldier!

above left: My family mean everything to me. Here I am with my partner Nic, our daughter Annabella and my stepdaughter Lauren, on holiday in 2005.

above right: Booted and suited… Here I am with Johnny Fast Hands, centre, and Big John, right, on John's wedding day.

below: Hired muscle… Me, Kev Webster, centre, and Big Dave Ferris, right.

Above left: Mike Tyson reckoned former Irish champion Joe Egan, right, was 'The Toughest White Man on the Planet'. Joe's a great fella and a great friend. He's a man I really look up to and admire.

Above right: My close pal Bryn Robertson and I cross Tower Bridge during the 2000 London Marathon.

Below: In San Francisco with mates Harry Holland, Dave Lewis, Danny the Mex and Alan the Hairdresser. Behind us is the island prison Alcatraz – and that's as close as I ever want to be to a place like that!

above: This picture was taken when Kostya Tsyzu came to Britain to fight Ricky Hatton. ...n left with Kostya's trainer Johnny Lewis – who is probably the best Australian trainer ...the business – Big Dave Ferris and Kev Webster.

below: Back row, left to right, Paul Biggs, me, Kev Webster and Big Dave Ferris ...ovided security for Kostya Tsyzu, front right, while he was in Britain to fight Ricky ...atton, front left. Ricky beat Kostya to take his IBF welterweight title.

My tragic fight versus Chris Henry; a
tough nut to crack, I was understandably
pleased to beat him, as was my trainer
Lenny, but my celebrations soon turned to
horror as it became clear that Chris was in
serious trouble on the canvas. Chris lost
consciousness and was rushed to hospital
where a blood clot to the brain was
diagnosed. Ringside safety measures have
been much improved since this incident.

To Nick.
Ruff. Ruff
& Read~1

Best Wishes
Milky.

Above: Didn't I do well! This is the picture I sent to my mate Nick Cole after I won the Southern Area title in 1997. I signed the picture Milky because of my ring nickname, The Milky Bar Kid.

Below: Happier times. Young boxer Lee Georgio and my trainer Lenny Butcher join in the celebrations after I won the vacant Southern Area title following my rematch against Kevin Mitchell in Barking in February 1999. Unfortunately, the wonderful relationship I had with Lenny was left in tatters after I was attacked in the Five Star Gymnasium.

Bruce Scott was one of the toughest fellas I've ever had to share a ring with.

I said, 'I didn't like you the first time I met you, coming over here and bigging it up. If you carry on I'll iron you out! Don't ever talk to me like that again. Have a bit of fuckin' respect!'

Aussie Dave looked flabbergasted. 'Come outside,' he said. 'We'll talk about it.'

That wasn't such a clever thing to say to me. 'Come outside' to me is an invitation for a ruck.

'Come outside with you? I'll chuck you over the balcony you little mug!'

Paul hurried over to Aussie Dave. 'I don't know what you've said, but you'd better stop 'cos this is what he's paid to do.' Paul managed to quickly calm me down. I went over to Ronnie and Carrie and stood by them for a while. 'What's going on?' they asked.

The next thing I knew Glenn Jennings was coming over to me, accompanied by Aussie Dave. 'What's going on between you two?' he demanded. Aussie Dave replied, 'I just asked him to do something and he *abused* me.'

I boiled over again. I told him I was going to iron him out if he didn't fuck off. He should do himself a favour and get out of my sight.

While all this had been going on, conversation in the ballroom had halted and everyone was looking in my direction. Glenn offered a few words of wisdom: 'I think you'd better walk away Dave.'

Sensible advice.

Afterwards I went downstairs to the foyer to get a cup of coffee. After a while Ricky and his folks left and some of Kostya's people wandered into the foyer. 'Bloody hell Dom,' said one of them, 'I thought they only spoke like that in *Lock, Stock and Two Smoking Barrels*!' Dr Bill turned up. 'Have you calmed down yet Dom, 'cos Dave wants a word.'

'I'm really sorry Dom, I shouldn't have spoken to you like that,' he said. He offered me his hand and we shook on it. 'I'm sorry too,' I said. 'It was very unprofessional of me.'

I also minded Prince Naseem Hamed when he boxed Paul Ingle at the MEN Arena in Manchester a few years back. I know some people think he's just flash, but Naz is a really nice guy. I flew out to Las Vegas in April 2001 with some mates – not to mind Naz though – and we saw him lose his IBO featherweight title at the MGM Grand Hotel by way of a points decision to Marco Antonio Barrera.

Naz was a real gent. He'd supplied me and my mates Dave Lewis, Danny the Mex and Alan the Hairdresser with some brilliant tickets for the fight – the best we'd ever had.

Danny's a top bloke – a bit of a character, as is his dad Brian, who we call The Fox. They're unbelievable guys, generous to a fault. Danny and me have known each other for around ten years. If I remember correctly, we first met in a gym and we've been friends ever since. He's well respected because he's a decent man. A business man in fact. He may not be big physically, but he's got a lot of bottle, he won't take shit from anybody. He trains regularly and, generally, keeps himself in pretty good shape.

Alan, well he's a really nice bloke who's been there for me through thick and thin. I love the guy and we have such a laugh together whenever we meet up which, sad to say, isn't often enough. As for Dave, well, later in my boxing career he became my manager. He's a smashing bloke of whom you will read more about later.

We'd flown out to spend a few days in America while taking in Naz's fight. On the way out we bumped into a chap called Harry Holland, a really nice fella who was a member of Audley Harrison's management team. He's also a bit-part actor who can often be seen on BBC TV's soap *EastEnders*. He's usually got a non-speaking part sitting around in the Queen Vic pub or working as a market stallholder.

En-route to Vegas we stopped off in San Francisco and found a really nice seafood restaurant near Pier 66. Harry doesn't normally drink but we were managing to get him a bit pissed as we all tucked into our lobsters and crabs. We were all sitting at a table next to a huge bay window.

'You know what,' said Harry, 'I'd love to see Alcatraz (the prison island) and the Golden Gate Bridge while we're here.'

I hadn't even thought of that but could appreciate they could be worth a look. As I poured myself another glass of wine I looked out of the window.

'Dave, what's that?' I asked as I looked at this huge building right opposite the restaurant.

'That's Alcatraz, you muppet!'

Then I looked further round outside the window and there in all its glory stood the Golden Gate Bridge. Harry's wishes had been granted without him even having to leave his seat.

I have to say though, that was as near as I'd ever want to be to a place like Alcatraz. Give me a classy restaurant, a glass of wine and some lobster anytime.

After Naz's fight we all went into an adjacent bar in the MGM Grand with some of Naz's people. Obviously the mood was rather sombre as Naz had lost for the first time in his career.

We all sat around having a few drinks, then Danny and Alan went up to the bar to get some more. From our table I became aware of a bit of banter going on at the bar area which was beginning to get a bit heated. It seems the barman wasn't too happy with the speed Danny had been ordering the drinks. He thought he should hurry up and get on with it. Something was said between them and then Alan chipped in too.

'So you're the funny guy are you?' said the barman to Alan. Then he gave Danny his change and, as he was a bit pissed off with him, Danny gave him back a dime and told him to get a new haircut. Obviously, that led to a row and, even more obviously, I got up, wandered over, and joined in.

As a consequence, the security people came hurrying over towards us – all armed with guns. One of them, a woman, drew her gun and pointed it in our direction. She ordered us to be quiet and to stand back.

'Hold on,' I said, 'We only came over to see the fight and this guy's out of order.' But she didn't want to know and told us we would have to leave. As she led us away she told us that it had been the fourth time that evening someone had had problems with that particular barman and that she'd had no option other than to diffuse the situation and that it would be okay if we wanted to come back the next day.

We'd planned to go to the post-fight party. As we'd been staying at a hotel on the opposite side of the Vegas Strip, The Excalibur, I decided it wouldn't take me long to run back to my room, to get changed, and to run back again. Alan and Danny said they'd wait at the MGM, so I hurried off. As I was running down the pavement – or should I say sidewalk – along the Strip I ran between two guys and accidentally brushed against one of them.

'Sorry mate!' I called out as I continued on my way.

Behind me I heard a voice, 'Mind where you're going, asshole!'

If you've ever seen a cartoon character running along and skidding to a complete stop, that's exactly what happened. I turned around.

'What did you say?'

One of them squared up to me but, before he could even think about saying anything else, a left hook laid him right out. His mate wasn't having that and he came at me too so I had to put him down as well. So there they were, one of them laid right out, the other sitting on his arse and groaning. Shit, I thought, I'd better clear off before someone calls the cops. With that I ran on back to my room to get changed.

On the way back to the MGM I was running along the opposite side of the Strip and watched as the two guys were being helped to their feet. That aside, the trip to Vegas turned out to be an amazing experience.

I bumped into Naz again in December 2005 when Audley Harrison was to fight Danny Williams for the Commonwealth heavyweight title at London's ExCel Arena. I walked Danny out to the ring. After I'd seen him safely there it was suggested I should also escort Harrison. Sorry, but no way. I couldn't be bothered. I just don't like the man. To my mind he's brought nothing to the table – a fact noticed by all the fans and television viewers who witnessed this fight when, after nine boring rounds, Danny put Harrison on his arse and, eventually, won on points.

Harrison hasn't the heart to make it big as a pro. After getting up in the tenth he'd hurt Danny in the next round but couldn't follow it up. Why didn't he try doing that in the first place? As far as I can see, he'll never have what it takes to win a worthwhile world title.

Chapter Six

A LOOSE CANNON

Over the following few pages I'll be revealing some of the mindless thuggery I've been involved in. That's not to glorify my violent lifestyle but, if people are to accept my desire to change for the better, they need to see how badly I've behaved in order to realise the scale of the challenge facing me if I am to successfully turn my life around. This, if you like, is my Everest.

For a period of around eight years I was a truly horrible person. I guess the curly-haired, fat, four-eyed teenager had set out to prove a point, wanting to create a reputation because he didn't feel he fitted in. I was always getting involved in other people's problems. Problems that often had absolutely nothing to do with me. I'm no angel, that's clear, but I got as close to the Devil as I could ever get.

I'd always known that I only had to throw just one clean punch to iron somebody out. That way it wouldn't be me rolling around on the ground. That's not to say I'd have knocked them out every time but, at least, they'd be sitting on their arse. My right hand is the strongest punch I throw but, if I connect with a left hook, no doubt about it, they're going down. I'd say to be on the end of one of my left hooks would be akin to being walloped by a bloody great hammer because, once I let it go, I can't stop it. With that knowledge I had no fear going into dangerous situations.

Just stupidity.

Looking back, the person I hurt the most was myself.

There have been so many incidents where trouble has followed me around or when I have just gone out in search of it. Just before I began working the doors, I was in a bar in Tottenham with a friend. There were a load of black geezers in there and my mate had a row with one of them. Before long it was clear they were trying to intimidate us. They were all men and, by comparison, I guess we were still boys.

My mate suggested we should leave and I agreed but my ego and determination not to be seen as a wimp got the better of me and, as we passed this huge doorman, I gave him a huge overhead right chop to the throat. He went straight down onto the floor and was rolling around. We just legged it while we could. In my mind, it was something I just had to do. I had to prove to myself that I had the bottle to do it.

In October 1998 I suffered a rarity. Defeat in the boxing ring. My promoter had pulled me out of the contest at the end of the fifth round because I'd become unwell and dizzy. More on that later. However, it really hurt my pride and, true to form, I had to go out to prove to myself, yet again, that I still had the bottle for a good old tear up.

A while later, Johnny Fast Hands, Big John and I were working the doors at a beer festival in Battersea and, true to form, I was deliberately putting myself into some decidedly dodgy situations. I was putting myself up on offer. Any sign of aggro and I was there, willing it on.

Of course, it all kicked off again, with me at the hub of it all. I was being unnecessarily heavy-handed with people, even instigating situations. It was like all I wanted to do was to pour petrol onto a fire. Okay, so I proved I still had the bottle – probably far too much for my own good – but my behaviour that day was no better than stupidity.

Shortly afterwards, still with this massive chip on my shoulder, I was in a nightclub. When I popped into the toilets I met three Asian geezers who, as far as I could see, had decided to wind me up. BANG, BANG, BANG – I beat the granny out of the lot of them. I really lost the plot.

Although I never actually instigated this particular situation, as soon as they'd provoked me, the writing was on the wall for them. I had so much anger inside me that I needed to let out.

Well, they got all of it.

Over the years I've been to some really beautiful places. Shortly before my infamous contest against Audley Harrison in 2002, Paul and I found ourselves in Marbella, Spain, looking after this rich fella (who, for the purposes of this book I'll call Tom), who was having a bit of aggro. Paul and me were there to help sort out a £100,000 debt he was owed.

This turned out to be a heavy duty job and, for our own peace of mind, we were advised to go tooled up. Paul was even offered a 9mm Walther PPK, while I was offered the use of a 9mm Colt 45. Yes, it was heavy stuff. Out there, in that circle they make their own rules.

One night, Paul, me and Tom, went into a bar for a drink where Tom ended up having a row with another bloke and Tom promptly chinned him. I decided I'd try to chuck him over the balcony. There was probably a drop of around 20ft the other side and the guy was hanging on for dear life, but I was interrupted when the doormen intervened and pulled us apart. They then led the fella away from us and started to ask us what had been going on. I told them we were there to look after Tom and that they should chuck the fella out, but they refused. So I decided to do the job myself. I went over to him and a decent right hook laid him right out. That's when it all kicked off and when all the doormen joined in too.

One of them came over and had a go at Paul who promptly chinned him. Quick as a flash, I jumped over a table, pushed Paul behind me and began chinning anyone who came near me. Another doorman came rushing up towards us. I caught him with a cracker but the guy still managed to chin me and my head spun right round. Paul got straight back into the action by jumping over a table and hitting him. By now, there were around five more doormen about to join in – and they all had truncheons. Suddenly, Paul took a whack and went down and everyone else piled in. Then I noticed that somebody with a truncheon around their throat was being dragged away. It was Paul and he was almost unconscious. I managed to get the truncheon away from the doorman and pulled Paul away from him, getting a tremendous bashing from the other truncheons as I did so.

I pulled Paul into a drinking area where there was not so much space, where I felt the doormen would have more difficulty in getting to us. Paul's head had been split open and, in effect, we were cornered. However, Paul soon came to his senses and we agreed that there was no way they were going to take us without a fight and we surged forward straight into them. One of them adopted a kickboxing stance. We quickly sized each other up but, before he could do anything, I'd done him with a left hook. At this point the remaining doormen changed tactics and decided that, rather than continuing the ruck, they would try to calm the situation down.

Eventually, we got down to some form of dialogue. 'What's happening now, mate?' I asked the big one. 'Look, I know how this works, 'cos this is my job back home.'

'Look mate,' he said, 'We've gotta ask you to leave 'cos we just can't be having this in here. This is a nightclub and you're scaring people who have only come here to have a good time.'

We agreed to leave quietly but, I have to say that had we had the guns on us at the time, bearing in mind the gravity of the situation in there, there's every possibility they may have been used and we could have ended up on a murder charge.

After this incident, we remained in Marbella for another two weeks. We'd stayed in a five-star hotel and walked away with a couple of grand each in our pockets. To me, the whole experience had been fun.

Now you tell me, is that normal?

Of course, having a gun isn't the same as making out you've got one but, as The Captain and I found out, it's handy to call people's bluff from time to time. We'd gone into a Turkish drinking den to collect a bad debt. Eventually, the geezer in there admitted he owed the cash so The Captain took him downstairs to continue the negotiations in the office. I was left to guard the top of the stairs so they weren't disturbed. Meanwhile, all eyes were on me and, to tell the truth, some of those guys looked a bit handy.

Then one of their telephones rang. I told him not to

answer it because I couldn't allow anyone to call out for back-up. The guy got a bit stroppy so I took the phone off him. 'Are you trying to be funny?' I said, and gently patted my pocket. It did the trick. I'd implied I was carrying a shooter and there was no way I was going to let them think otherwise. Suddenly, from a situation where I'd been heavily outnumbered, it looked as though they were all shitting themselves. I told them all to sit still where they were and they duly obliged.

It was around ten to 15 minutes before The Captain emerged from the office downstairs but it seemed a lot longer. Nevertheless, we got out safely and the job was done.

I've rarely had to go out tooled up or had to get particularly heavy in this line of work, but sometimes it is necessary. Of course, for some people operating in these sort of circles, it's unlikely they would ever call the Old Bill because they wouldn't want to draw any unwelcome attention to themselves.

The only people I've ever hurt in this sort of work deserved it – usually they were people with reputations of their own. Sometimes I just had to fight fire with fire. Whether or not I went out tooled up depended on the type of job or situation I'd be dealing with on the day. My thing was either a knuckleduster or a blade, but they'd only actually be used in situations when I'd found myself outnumbered because, at that stage, you just can't afford to fuck about.

There have been occasions when I've had to collect debts from shady car dealers but, when I've turned up, they'd arranged for half a dozen heavies to be there to welcome me. It was always obvious why they were there so I couldn't waste my shots if I needed to take any of them out. That's when the knuckleduster came in handy but, I stress, it was only used occasionally.

As for the blade, well, maybe a couple of times. Trouble is, it's not something you can threaten to use. If you pull it out, you've gotta use it, and be quick about it because, if you don't get them, they get you. Yet I was always aware of the fact that if I used the blade I'd be treading a very fine line. If I'd ever nicked someone's artery, I could well have ended up facing a murder charge.

It was before all my real troubles, probably around 1998, that me, Big John and another mate, Nick Cole, took one of our first holidays together in Tenerife. Nick is such a nice guy. If my own daughter, when she's old enough, was to come home with a lad like Nick, I'd be more than happy. Sometimes he's so laid back his head rubs on the floor. I've known him and his parents Jackie and Bill and his brother and sister Jordana and Will for a while now and they're a really nice family.

Big John, Nick and me decided to have a night on the town and, as we made our way along the infamous Strip, we were practically legless by the time we found ourselves outside a McDonald's restaurant. Suddenly,

Nick said, 'Hey Dom, look over there, there's a fight!' A couple of Lookie Lookie men – the guys over there who are always trying to sell you watches and so on – were bashing up a couple of English lads. Even though it was none of our business, we were straight over.

'Are you alright?' I said to one of the English lads. He seemed very relieved to see us. I told one of the Lookie Lookie men to do himself a favour and to fuck off then, BANG, he'd hit me right on the chin. Nick reckoned afterwards that the force turned my head right round but, once I'd screwed it back on, I came back with a belter and laid the guy right out. The other Lookie Lookie man cleared off and I thought that was the end of it but, within moments, we found ourselves surrounded by a gang of them and they were moving in on us.

Shit, what had I done?

Now Big John can really handle himself but, when I looked around, he was on the ground and getting a good kicking. But they couldn't keep him down. Like Frankenstein, he sat up, then jumped to his feet. Even though he was so pissed, he was still able to shrug them off, and then he proceeded to knock them all over the place.

Meanwhile, I found myself being swung around. All I could think was 'don't go down, don't go down!' I think there were around three of them trying to kick and punch me and one of them managed to connect with a hard kick right onto my chin. I adopted a boxing stance. 'Come on then!'

A load of girls standing around outside McDonald's were calling out to Nick, telling him to do something. 'They're okay,' he said, 'They're just enjoying themselves!'

Seizing an opportunity, I got down as low as I could and pulled an upper cut as hard as I could into the bollocks of one of the guys setting on me. He collapsed squealing like mad in agony.

At this stage I felt I was beginning to get on top of the situation; that is until I felt these arms being wrapped so tightly around me I couldn't move. Who on earth had the strength to do that?

It was Big John. He pulled me out from the middle of the mêlée, lifted me up in front of him, and turned his back to shield me.

We regrouped. 'Let 'em have it!' At this point, one of the geezers pulled out a dirty great chain and started trying to hit me round the head with it. Rather than backing off, I went towards him. He was the last one still fighting but, when he turned to run off, I knocked him out. His mates hurried to pick him up and, between them, they all managed to pile into a couple of small cars and pissed off.

We decided to celebrate with a burger in McDonald's but, because we were all covered in blood, the security men, all armed with batons, wouldn't let us in. I suppose we should have just been glad to come out of it all in one piece. In fact, I reckon we all did pretty well considering how pissed we'd been at the time.

It was usually different if I spent time in Tenerife with a good friend of mine, Bryn Robertson and his wife Sarah. It is always much quieter because Bryn doesn't drink alcohol so we don't tend to hit the bars so much. We prefer to go to the other side of the island where the scenery is absolutely beautiful.

One year, I went to stay with Bryn and Sarah at their villa for a couple of weeks, although after the first week, Bryn and Sarah had planned to return to England. Nevertheless, they left me some keys so I could come and go as I wished the following week. That was the week Danny the Mex and me spent down The Strip in the bars and I suppose, with our track record, trouble was never going to be too far away.

While we were there we bumped into a guy called Sweeney, I can't remember his Christian name. He told us he was the unlicensed heavyweight champion of the island which, basically, means jack shit. Me being me, I train wherever I go, so I offered him the chance to have a move around in the gym the next day. 'I won't spar with you,' he said, 'but I know this really big African guy who will.' I told him I only wanted to keep fit, I wasn't looking to knock anyone out.

Around 3am, I found myself in a bar with Danny and a chap we called Cliffy, which, I gather, is not his real name. He was staying out there because he was still wanted by the police in England. I have to say he turned out to be quite a character in his own right.

Sweeney came in with a tasty looking bird. Also in the bar at the time were half a dozen northern fellas who were eyeing up Sweeney's bird and making lewd comments about her.

After a while, Sweeney came over to us and said he reckoned they needed teaching a lesson, obviously expecting us to help him out but, when I looked around, the northerners had vanished so I told him not to worry about it. A little later, Danny, Cliffy and me moved to a neighbouring bar and we stood around in the VIP area adjacent to a big dance floor. Then Sweeney turned up. 'Those northerners are back.' 'Okay,' I said. 'I haven't come in here for any aggro but if you do what you want to do I'll back you up.' Quite why I agreed to get involved at all, I don't know. Prior to his return to England Bryn had told me I should calm down and stay out of trouble.

Danny and Cliffy were completely unaware of what was going on when I told Sweeney to go over to the northerners and to tell them we'd sort it out in the toilet, but Sweeney started twitching like a frightened bird. That gave me the hump because he was making me look a prat, so I approached the northerners for a closer look.

The first one I came to was humungous. He didn't seem to have a neck and he was covered in tattoos. Another was about my size, the others were pretty big but just a bunch of idiots. As he walked past me, the biggest one barged into me. He was testing me out. I told Sweeney that, if he didn't do something, I would and told him to watch my back. I touched the big guy on the back and asked him if he had a problem with Sweeney.

'Yeah, I fuckin' have.'

So I punched his lights out. Then one of his mates had a go and I punched his lights out too, although this time it took two punches to do so. Must have been losing my touch. Suddenly, I was being jumped on so I had to start swinging.

Back in the VIP area, Cliffy noticed the commotion. 'Look over there Danny, that guy can really have a go, can't he?'

'You're right mate, that's Dominic!'

Within seconds, they'd come steaming in to help me, which was just as well as Sweeney was nowhere to be seen – well done champ!

As I was belting them out, Danny and Cliffy started chucking them out until we got down to the last one. He'd been the one pecking away at me all the way through.

'I don't want any trouble mate!'

Too late. He even got a kicking for good measure.

It seems there's always something happening whenever I go to Tenerife. I was there again in 2000 with a few mates, including my manager Dave Lewis. We went into a famous bar on The Strip which I won't name because it's owned by a friend of mine. We were all having a bit of a laugh around the pool table which was great for me because this was at a time I'd been experiencing several episodes of paranoia.

Everything was fine until a young, chunky-looking fella entered the room. He began to stare at me, so much so it made me feel pretty uncomfortable. I asked Dave what he reckoned it was all about, but he said he had no idea.

The fella continued to watch my every move. I didn't like what was happening so I decided to tuck myself away in a corner more out of sight, but still I was being stared at and it was really bugging me. Then he got up from his seat and moved towards the bar. He sat down. By now he was just a matter of feet away from me and I could see what looked like metal keys between his fingers. I moved away again towards one of my mates who didn't like the look of what was happening either.

Fuck this, I thought. I'd had enough. I walked around the pool table and up to the bloke. 'Have you got a problem?' I bust a pool cue over his head. He dropped onto the floor.

That'll teach him.

Somebody dragged him outside and Dave, me and the lads remained in the bar for a few more drinks. Then another couple of fellas I knew came in. 'Do you know anyone who can get any coke for us?' they asked. I told them I'd speak to my mate who owned the bar but, when I spoke to him, he had a go that I'd been at it again. 'This is my bar and you're giving it a bad name.' I apologised then asked him if he knew anyone who could get their hands on some coke.

'What are you like, you prat! You've just knocked out my bloody dealer!'

We found him outside a while later. 'Look mate,' I said. 'I apologise.'

'Bloody hell, mate,' he replied, 'I only wanted your autograph, I couldn't believe it was you.'

Another punch-up in the same bar ended up with me being stabbed. There were four of us in there at the time. We were sitting around, laughing and joking, all of us pretty well paralytic. Then these birds turned up and one of my mates, a reasonably good-looking fella who's into bodybuilding, went to sit with them and started chatting them up.

Then a load of local geezers turned up and we could see straight away they had the hump with my mate. After a while, he got up to go to the toilet. The locals, who were sitting near us, had no idea we knew the object of their ire. One of them, a little geezer, nudged his mate, pointed at our mate and said, 'He's going into the toilets, we can sort him out in there.'

As his mate stood up to follow our mate into the toilets I stood up and landed one right on his chin. He went down like a pack of cards. Then I heard the smashing of glass and, before I could get out of the way, the little geezer had stuck the end of a broken bottle into my right hand. My instant reaction was a left hook. Then, out of the corner of my eye I thought I saw another bottle coming towards me so I spun round and twice clobbered the guy to my side. Trouble was, it was one of my mates and, as I hit him, one of his teeth came right through his lip and he slumped to the floor. Then our mate emerged from the toilets, quite unaware of what had been going on.

It looked like a scene from a bar-room brawl in a western. The music stopped, the DJ started packing up his equipment, and all the lights came on.

I reached down to grip the collar of my mate's shirt and pulled him up. 'Come on mate,' I said, 'Wake up.'

In 2002, Johnny Fast Hands and me were at Blue Mondays in Buckhurst Hill, a bar we often frequented. As we were chatting, a guy I've known well for years came in with around ten other fellas. He's now a well-known television actor who has starred in, amongst others, *The Bill*, *Hollyoaks*, and *Footballers' Wives*. I stood up to greet him with one of my customary big hugs. 'Hello mate, are you all right?'

'Whoa!' he said, raising his arms as if he didn't want me to crumple his fancy suit. Then he turned away from me as if he felt he was now too famous to be associated with the likes of me. That upset me a lot.

'Oi, don't get monkey with me,' I said.

'What?'

'You fuckin' heard,' I said. 'If that's the way you want to be, the next programme you'll be in is *Casualty*. Do yourself a favour and fuck off!'

He returned to his mates and, after a short discussion, it looked as if they were going to leave. Johnny went up to him to explain. 'You've upset him,' he said. 'Look, it's up to you. If you want to hang about, fine, but you know what will happen.'

Okay, so the guy got a bit flash. So what? To be honest, the way I was at the time, after a few drinks, I could be a pretty horrible person myself.

Not all of my mates are into fighting. One of them, Alan the Hairdresser, isn't into it at all, which is one reason I found myself dragged into another violent confrontation. Like most of my mates, Alan is a football fan. Most of my mates are either Tottenham or Arsenal fans and, on this particular night, four of them had popped into a local pub for a drink. Late that night I received a telephone call from Tan and Teeth – a mate of mine who's got a permanent tan and big teeth, believe it or not. Tan's a little sod. He upsets an awful lot of people because he's not exactly shy when it comes to women. He'll nick anyone's bird given half the chance – a proper Casanova with all the banter. He just loves the birds, but it gets him into a whole load of trouble. That's why so many guys don't get on with him. He's a liability, but I like him all the same.

'Dom, we've got a problem,' said Tan.

'I don't really want to get involved, what's the matter. Who's with you?'

'Alan the Hairdresser.'

Up to that point I hadn't been too concerned because most of my mates can look after themselves, but Alan wasn't exactly a troublemaker. I asked Tan to put Alan on the phone and asked if he was okay. I could tell he was very worried about a situation developing in the pub so I told him I'd be there as soon as I could.

I jumped into the car and hurried towards the pub, picking up Paul on the way. I told him Tan had a problem.

'Oh, he can handle it,' said Paul.

'Alan's with him.'

'Right, let's be going.'

Within moments we'd pulled up outside the pub. Four of them were standing outside – Alan, Tan and two others. By now it was 11 at night and me and Paul hadn't driven over there just to have a conversation. Paul suggested he and me should go in one entrance of the pub and the others should return to the bar where they'd had the hassle through the other entrance.

Being local, it seemed just about everyone in the pub knew me, but they soon realised something was up when I just walked past them all saying hardly anything.

'What's going on?'

'Nothing, don't worry about it.'

Paul and me walked through the upper bar and down the steps into the lower bar where we could hear a load of guys taunting Alan, Tan and the others. I strode between them all.

'Who the fuckin' hell are y— ' BANG! He went flying across a table just as his mate came at me with a broken beer glass. I had to make short work of him before he could get me, so he went flying too.

The next thing I knew, I had someone's arms and legs wrapped around me. It was the manageress of the bar – she'd jumped onto my back! I shook her off me and, suddenly, all the guys that had originally rounded on me backed off.

But where was Paul?

When I went outside, I found him.

'What happened to you?' I asked.

'Sorry Dom, I couldn't get involved, they're all my mates in there.'

The following day I received a telephone call from a mate, Terry from Bermondsey, telling me that a couple of his mates had been knocked out at a pub the previous night.

'Oh yeah,' I said. 'Nothing to do with football was it?'

'Yeah, that's right. We're trying to find out who the geezer was. He's supposed to be a bit of a face but no-one's saying who he is.'

'I can tell you exactly who it was.'

'Who?'

'Me.'

The phone went quiet for a while. Then I heard him laughing.

'What happens now Terry, have we got a problem?' I asked.

'Dom, we'll never have a problem mate.'

I told him that if the geezers wanted to carry on, I was up for it. If they phoned me, we'd get it on but, when I did eventually meet up with them, even though they were football hooligans, I got on alright with them – and I even ended up doing a bit of work with them.

As I've mentioned, Alan's a good friend. When I fought Audley Harrison in July 2002 I was followed closely by the television cameramen as I entered the arena and my T-shirt had *Alan's Hairdressing* printed on the back. That was probably the best publicity his business has ever had.

I remember going out for a Sunday meal with The Tall Fella in a carvery when Alan walked in with a girlfriend. We decided we'd all like to sit together but couldn't get a table at this particular venue so we all moved on to another pub. We all sat down and were having a good time, enjoying a nice meal and drink together.

A couple of nights previously I'd had a bit of a falling out with a bloke who, I knew, often frequented the pub we were in. I told The Tall Fella that the only thing that could spoil the current atmosphere would be if that particular bloke was to turn up. After a while I paid a visit to the toilet. While I was in there, Alan's new girlfriend, who had never met me before, spoke to Alan about me. 'Dominic's not that bad at all. I've heard so many horror stories about him but he's as nice as pie.'

Alan agreed with her.

Then, lo and behold, who should walk into the pub but the fella I'd fallen out with! I know it was over something really stupid but, in my eyes, he'd been right out of order. I first noticed him as I emerged from the toilets and, let's just say, I wasn't over-pleased to see him again. He was a big lump, and it was obvious he'd seen me, but he made a point of ignoring me completely which, to my mind, was disrespectful. 'I'm not happy about this,' I said to The Tall Fella. Then, to rub it in, the bloke came over to our corner of the room and began talking to someone really near to us. Still he ignored me completely.

That did it. I stood up and said to Alan. 'I love Sundays! I'll be back in a minute.' Alan's heart must have sunk. He knew very well what the term I love Sundays meant – it was our saying of the time, always the precursor to a ruck. I stepped towards the fella and tapped him on the shoulder and, as he turned around, I nutted him and grabbed him by the throat. People were getting up to intervene but Alan was yelling out 'Don't touch him!' to warn them because he knew, had anyone even touched me at that moment, the chances were I'd knock them out. Instead they dragged the fella outside away from me.

Once I'd calmed down a little, the guy who owned the pub sat down next to me. I apologised for the incident, adding: 'But he was out of order'.

'You're fuckin' mad,' he replied.

As for Alan's girlfriend, she quickly realised the tales she'd originally heard about me weren't so far off the mark after all.

Last, but not least, was the occasion Nic and I had a bit of a row. My fault. It was late on New Year's Eve. I got the hump and decided to walk down the road to spend the night at a mate's house. But first of all I had to walk to the pub where he was working. Being New Year's Eve, he was on a late shift.

On the way I found myself walking down a remote country lane where I was approached by two big foreign-looking fellas. 'Got any money?' said one of them. Being in the middle of nowhere I assumed they were going to try to mug me so I bashed them both up.

Later, when I told Big John what had happened he suggested the fellas might have been wondering if I was okay and had been offering me some money to get home.

Who knows? It was just the drink in me I suppose.

So there you have it. The crazy world of Dominic Negus. Always up for a fight. Never one to back down whatever the circumstances. I'd been living in a world where only the strongest survived.

And where stupidity reigned.

I guess some right-minded, ordinary, decent people wouldn't even have picked up this book. Those who have – those who have stuck with it this far – will probably have a pretty low opinion of me by now but, believe it or not, one of my greatest desires is to be just like them. I want to change. I'm determined to do my best to become a decent family man who can hold his head up high in society.

Some may think I've been trying to glorify some of the less than savoury things I have done in the past but nothing could be further from the truth. There are already plenty of hard-man type books on the shelves.

The difference here is that while some of the other guys' books have revelled in what they've done, I'm truly ashamed of many of my past activities. This is my way of trying to get on with my life with a clean slate.

Let's be honest though, there are plenty of things I've done or been involved in in the past that will never see the light of day in print. Not a chance.

I never gave a toss about anyone or anything. I was always trying to show people my worth. Trouble was, they were the wrong kind of people. Respect and fear are two very different things, and it took me a long time to realise it. It's so much better to go into a place where people respect you rather than fear you.

And, of course, I'm well aware that all those years of throwing my weight around could come back to haunt me one day. I must have made so many enemies throughout my 'lost years' and I can never be sure that one of them may fancy having a pop back at me should the opportunity ever present itself. It's something I've given a lot of thought to, although I have to say, I try not to lose too much sleep over it.

What's done is done. That's the way I have to look at it. I can't change the past, can I? That means I've got to concentrate on whatever the future may hold for me. If I was to allow myself to become fearful of any revenge attacks, I reckon I would be too scared to open my own front door, and that's no way to live.

The aura of fear I managed to establish for myself was no good for me in the long run. If you have such an aura, before you know it, you're on the bully up

and doing and saying things to get what you want. I
found I could walk into a bar or club and never have
to buy a drink, or walk to the front of a queue at a
nightclub and be let straight in. Everybody knew my
name. I'd stand there with a drink in my hand,
surrounded by so-called friends, yet I was probably
the loneliest person in The Valley of Lost Souls. Of
course there were always places I could go for a quick
ego fix but, as the fix faded, the loneliness always
crept back in.

I remember looking in my bathroom mirror and
really not liking the man looking back at me. I had
become so distant from what I would call the real me.
When I got up each morning I had to stop for a
moment and think who I was going to be that day
depending on what I had to do. In the end, I just
became very lost. I was becoming what certain people
wanted me to be.

It got to the stage that I wasn't a nice person to be
around, a point driven home to me one day when I
received a telephone call from Bryn. As usual, I'd
been a bit ratty, but what Bryn had to say really
shook me, bearing in mind how close I felt to him.
'Dom, I really can't be around you for a while,' he
said. That really upset me because, out of everyone I
knew, he was probably one I looked up to more than
many. He's always told me the truth and, let's face it,
sometimes the truth hurts. 'Dom, you're becoming
too unpredictable. You make me feel uncomfortable,
flying off the handle and all that.' I didn't like what

he was saying and was crying down the telephone at the cruelty of his words. But, at the end of the day, he was so right.

When I look back at all the scrapes I've been in, well, to be honest, I can hardly believe I'm still here to tell the tale. In fact it's often been suggested I was some kind of gangster. Well, I can categorically say that I was *never* a gangster.

Just a bloody fool.

Chapter Seven

THE DARKEST DAYS

It was at the end of August 2003 when I was arrested in connection with an armed kidnapping. Heavy stuff.

I suppose I have to be very careful about how I describe the circumstances of my demise. I have a lot of enemies out there and have no desire to stir things up again, particularly after all the grief that followed my arrest. Let's just say there had been an altercation following a collision involving a car that I had access to, and the Old Bill reckoned that I looked a bit like the person who was allegedly responsible for forcing some guy into a car at gunpoint.

My arrest came soon after the plane I'd been in landed at Stansted airport. I'd just returned from Edinburgh where, with some friends and my boxing manager Dave Lewis, I'd been to my mate Danny Harrison's wedding. It had been a brilliant day, one of the best weddings I'd been to since Bryn married Sarah.

As the plane rolled to a halt I looked through the window and noticed a number of police cars outside. Obviously something wasn't right and a number of my travelling companions who were known to the police began to get the heeby jeebies. Me? I had no idea why they were there.

It took around 15 minutes before they would let anyone off the plane, although it seemed quite a bit longer. However, eventually we all began filing out. As we did so, a guy behind me, who I now know was one of three plain clothes police officers who had travelled on the plane, switched on his walkie talkie and said, 'We've got him. He's leaving the plane now.' I still had no idea he was referring to me.

However, it soon became apparent I was the target of their attentions. As I went down the steps to the tarmac I found myself surrounded by coppers carrying machine guns.

'Dominic Negus, I'm arresting you for the kidnapping of X.'

'What, who? I ain't done anything.'

My mates were totally gobsmacked by my arrest. Charlie, the young son of one of them, began to cry, 'What's going on?' His dad told him that the coppers were mates of mine and that I'd be going away to have a chat with them. I was taken to the police station at the airport. I told them I wanted to speak to my solicitor. The coppers took everything from me, including my shoes, and put me in a cell but, give them their dues, they treated me okay.

I decided I wasn't going to give them a hard time and tried to remain chirpy. Dom the joker. It didn't wash and, behind the smiles, I was thinking, 'What am I gonna do? I just want to get out of here.'

Outside the door I could hear people talking. I heard my name mentioned. They'd already taken my mobile phone. I told them my solicitor's number was on it. A copper popped his head round the door and asked me to come with him. He told me they'd phoned my solicitor but there was a message that he'd lost his phone and would get back to the caller as fast as he could!

'Shit, that's no good.'

Meanwhile, my travelling companions realised I was in big trouble and had arranged a solicitor on my behalf. I'm glad they chose the one they did because he was the bollocks. Top man. He phoned through. 'Hi, I'm Nick. I'll make this short and sweet. I'll be with you as quickly as I can. They're going to take you to Harlow police station now. Don't say anything because I still don't know exactly what's going on, but this is a very serious offence. You've been arrested for *armed* kidnapping.'

My head was spinning as I was taken to the cell. Then three National Crime Squad coppers turned up to see me. They had handcuffs, the sort the wearer can only hold their arms in a certain position. 'Listen fellas,' I said, 'I don't want the handcuffs, I ain't gonna do anything.' I was told the cuffs were not only for my protection but for theirs as well.

They put the cuffs on me. Then they drove me to Harlow in an unmarked police car. On one side of me was this skinny geezer and, on the other side, some bird I reckoned must have been a lesbian because whatever I said to her she looked like she wanted to spit at me. It's not as if I hadn't been trying to lighten the atmosphere. She just didn't want to know.

The other coppers in the car seemed to know just about everything about me boxing-wise, even though, by this time, my professional career was over and I was earning a few bob on the unlicensed circuit.

'You boxed so and so didn't you? Then you boxed so and so, blah, blah, blah.'

Next thing it was, 'How long has Dave Lewis been your manager?'

'Hold on, whoa! Listen, if you want to talk about me, go ahead, no problem. I ain't saying a fuckin' word about anybody else!'

Dave and me had booked our flights about three weeks earlier. I guess, since they'd been looking for me, my name must have popped up on some flight list on a computer somewhere. That's probably how they found me at the airport. Unbeknown to me, Dave had also been arrested. They took his bags and questioned him for a while, but didn't hang on to him.

When we arrived at Harlow police station my solicitor Nick came to see me. He's the only bloke I've ever met – he's only about five foot six – that I've ever sat in front of and been petrified of. The way he was talking, I thought I was going to be put away for ever. 'Dominic, there's a lot of evidence against you. It really doesn't look good.'

I asked him what could happen to me. He told me that, on a good day, I could be sentenced to up to eight years. On a bad day it could be up to 15.

The coppers took DNA swabs and wanted to take a picture of me but Nick said they couldn't. Then I was videoed for an identity parade. Apparently, there's no need to be there in person now, it's done electronically. The filming only took around ten seconds in total – 'Look straight ahead, turn to the right, back to the middle, turn to the left, back to the middle'. Nick and I were then permitted to sit down and select eight other people that vaguely resembled me in a series of videos for the line-up. By this point I'd learnt that three other men had also been arrested for the same offence.

Because I'd been arrested for an armed offence, the Old Bill had gone round to my flat in Havering-atte-Bower and had a good rummage around. They took a load of my stuff, including my computer. By now I was becoming increasingly worried.

However, it seemed a good number of the coppers in Harlow were into boxing. I told them I was due to have a world title fight against a German fella in Braintree, Essex. They seemed pretty interested and suggested they wouldn't mind coming along to watch. 'Any chance of a police discount?' I told them, if they were to take me out straight away and drop me off by the roundabout outside, I'd give them the tickets for nothing!

Even though I was questioned repeatedly, I'd only say 'no comment'. I was kept at Harlow for around ten hours before I was given unconditional bail. With my solicitor's prediction of up to 15 years inside, I was in a terrible state and decided to get a cab straight back to Nic's house – we weren't living together at this stage in our relationship – but, when I arrived, she wasn't in and the house was locked.

I decided to try to get in through the window but I couldn't do it. However, Nic had this habit of leaving the car keys in the car, so I jumped in it and drove to her mum Lorraine's house in Loughton. I rang the doorbell. I was so depressed, and desperate to see someone. When Lorraine opened the door I told her she was the best looking lady I'd ever seen and hugged her. 'Are you alright?' she asked. 'What's going on?'

I told her I could either tell her the truth or I couldn't, it was up to her. 'Tell me the truth.' I think Lorraine thought it was something to do with Nic's ex-boyfriend. She thought I may have hurt him – or worse. I explained what had been going on. I told Lorraine how I had promised her daughter everything but, in truth, I couldn't give her anything.

Lorraine, a brilliant Jewish lady, tried to reassure me that everything would be okay. 'It's going to be alright Dominic. I've said a prayer for you because we [Lorraine and Nic's stepdad John] know you are a good man. We don't care what you've done in the past, we've only seen what you've done for Nic.'

The day I was nicked marked the beginning of a steep downward spiral in my life that lasted for the next five months. It was hell. I began drinking heavily and doing a bit of cocaine two or three times a week in an effort to blot everything out of my mind. I can't say I was a virgin to coke but, while I'd been training professionally, I hadn't been involved with it at all. It was so easy to get hold of. Being a regular in the local bars, everyone seemed to be offering me coke or buying me drinks or whatever. I guess they just wanted to keep me sweet.

The coke, though, didn't make me feel any better. I was taking it to help me sober up, to straighten me out. Over the coming weeks, it only served to get me into even more trouble. Nor could I handle the booze. It's not that I was falling over or anything like that, it's just that it used to fire me up. It got so bad I couldn't think straight. I was damaged goods. I became far too paranoid to stay at Nic's house. I was convinced the Old Bill would be coming to get me at any time. Christmas was looming and I was convinced it would be the last one I'd spend on the outside for a good number of years.

I suppose I went for three weeks without any sleep. Most nights I found myself in a bar. One night I was watching a football match on a TV in a bar and started to doze, but I was so paranoid, thinking the police were coming, or that people were out to get me, that I didn't let myself fall asleep.

Looking back, I feel sorry for my mate Matty who I was staying with at the time. I thought I'd had it all sussed. I reckoned that, if the Old Bill were going to come for me, they'd probably come around half past six one morning and I'd worked out how I'd get to the gate before they could grab me. It's mad, the way my head was. The booze and cocaine were really doing me in.

Enzo Veuto is another good friend. We've stuck by each other through thick and thin over the years. He's a short Italian fella about ten years older than me. Unlike many of my friends he's not a rucker by any means. Enzo sells a few cars or a bit of clothing here and there, although he's a plumber by trade. Sometimes he rubs people up the wrong way, but we've always got on well. After he got divorced I went to stay at his place for a year or so, even though we're like chalk and cheese.

While waiting for the court case to come up, I spotted Enzo's son doing a paper round and asked him if he would get his dad to call me. Enzo phoned and we spent ages chatting. He was a great support to me. Sometimes, Enzo gets low too, so I like to be there for him, just as he was for me.

Enzo and me reckoned the Old Bill were watching me and tried to make a joke of it to lighten things up. We went into the Oxfam shop in Epping and I bought myself a wig, glasses, an old tweed jacket and a pair of trousers that were way too short. We had a bit of a laugh, then walked into Blue Mondays, the bar in

Buckhurst Hill where Nic worked. I used to go there most days, but no-one recognised me, not even Nic. Then the rumours started flying around – Dominic's lost the plot. For Christ's sake – it was a JOKE!

All the pressure was causing strain between me and Nic. One night, after we'd had a bit of a row, Nic decided she'd rather sleep in Lauren's room. Fuck that, I thought. If I'm going to sleep on my own I'd rather stay at a mate's house. I phoned him up to ask if I could stay over. No problem.

At the time I was driving around in another mate's car, a brand new red Volkswagen Golf. I jumped in it and proceeded to drive off the estate where Nic lived to my friend's place. In front of me, walking very slowly in the middle of the road, were two huge geezers, one black, one white. They'd decided it would be fun to be a pain in the arse and to slow up any traffic. It was obvious they had no intention of moving aside.

Bearing in mind all my problems at the time, and the fact I had the right hump after rowing with Nic, this wasn't exactly a good time to wind me up. I opened the car window and called out to them, 'Do me a favour lads, get out the way.'

'Oh yeah?'

'Just fuckin' move!'

They didn't so I just decided I'd squeeze past them. As I did so, one spat on the car, the other tried to kick it. I pulled over to the side of the road and stopped.

'What do you think you're fuckin' doing? I said.

117

'Oh, think you're tough do ya?' said the white guy. He didn't have time to say anything else because I hit him with a right hander and he was sitting on his arse. The black fella adopted a boxing stance. 'Come on then,' he said.

I looked up at the sky and said, 'Thank you.' Anyone who's ever watched me boxing will know that, prior to the start of any fight, I always crossed myself. Part of my Catholic upbringing. Seeing this guy adopt the stance pleased me because at least I knew he wasn't going to try and stab me. He wanted to fight.

I'm a boxer but, when I'm living my life on the streets, well it's bollocks to the Queensberry Rules. That's probably why I'm still here and some people aren't. I took a step to the left and hit him right on the chin with what was probably one of the best left hooks I've ever delivered. He went flying. When I drove off they were both lying in the road with birds flying around their heads tweeting.

The next day I received a telephone call from a mate who lived on the estate where the incident took place. He told me a couple of bullies from the estate had been beaten up the night before. The bloke who did it had been driving a new Volkswagen Golf. If I found out who it was, would I thank him for putting the bastards in their place?

It was around this time a friend of mine, a property dealer, was experiencing a few difficulties in Cyprus where he was having some buildings put up. He wanted me to fly over to give him a bit of support after some heavies over there had been trying to muscle in on him. He booked the flights and I was due to leave from Heathrow. I told Nic I'd be away, but only for the weekend, to do some work. At the airport my bags went through the metal detecting machine without any problems and I got through the security check but, as I walked into the duty free shop, I was approached by two geezers who pulled me to one side.

Old Bill. Just what I needed, particularly considering the paranoia I'd been experiencing at the time. They wanted to check my passport, and I showed them my bail sheet. I told them I'd already spoken to my solicitor and that I'd told him where I was going. 'Ah,' said one of them, looking at my passport. 'So you're Dominic Negus the fighter.'

'Yeah, that's right. Is that good or bad then?'

'Depends on which end you're standing, doesn't it? Look, we already knew it was you.'

'How did you know I was coming through?'

'Flight plan.'

Maybe they'd thought I was going to leg it because northern Cyprus doesn't have an extradition treaty but, after a few questions, they let me on my way. After that I had three nice days in the sun. I was given all my expenses and 500 quid on top.

On my arrival, my friend was really worried about what had been going on. I told him that if things were as bad as he was saying, well, I was only a one-man band. If he was right in his assessment of the situation,

I reckoned it wouldn't be too long before the both of us would be at the bottom of one of the holes he'd had dug out for the foundations of his building. It hadn't helped matters too much either that he'd told the guys who I was and that he'd sent for me to back him up. I wasn't too happy about that because it didn't give me too much room to manoeuvre.

It was easy money as it turned out. I shadowed my mate wherever he went and kept a close eye on him, and the pair of us went to a pre-arranged meeting with the guys he was so worried about. To be honest, I think my mate may have over-reacted because, when I met up with them, they weren't too bad after all. In fact, they were fine with me too. I told my mate that, maybe, he'd got the wrong end of the stick, that he should calm down and that everything would be okay, even though they'd put him under a bit of pressure earlier on.

At the end of the day, property business can be big business. Invariably, there's a lot of money involved and everyone concerned wants to make sure their money is safe and that they get as much as they can for it.

It had been a good trip but the incident at the airport on the way out had reinforced my obsession that the Old Bill were watching me all the time and that they would soon be coming after me.

On my return, in an effort to get the Old Bill of my back for a while, I went to stay with friend and training partner Wayne Cummings.

It was while I was at Wayne's that I first thought about doing it.

I *knew* they were going to come for me. I just *knew*. I *knew* they'd probably break the door down in the early hours and come and get me. That's what they'd do. But I had a plan. By the time they got in, I'd be gone.

I'd be dead.

Unsurprisingly, my relationship with Nic had been under considerable strain since I'd made an effort to put some distance between us. I wanted to see her but couldn't face putting her through everything that had been happening at the time. I knew the police were keeping a close eye on me and my associates, and that they'd been going round asking questions about me. Looking back, I just praise God that He made Nic see I was worth all the aggro that I was putting her and her family through at the time.

While I'd been staying at Wayne's I'd been sleeping on the sofa in his lounge. I just sat there and waited. Waited for Wayne to go up to bed. At last he went upstairs. Finally, it was time to sort things out once and for all. They couldn't get me now.

I went into the kitchen and had a good rummage around to see what I could use. I found a knife.

That'll do.

Within moments I was back in the lounge and was slashing away at my wrists and there was claret was going all over the place. I wrapped myself in a duvet and laid down. For a while I just watched the blood pouring from the wounds. This ain't so bad, I thought, and closed my eyes. It'll soon be over.

In the morning, the duvet was soaked in blood – and I woke up.

That's it. Still alive.

'What have I done? What have I done?'

I bandaged my wounds with tea towels, cleaned up all the mess I'd made, and went in to Wayne's bedroom. As soon as he saw the blood he said, 'I might have bloody well known you'd do something like this!' He was in total shock. Had he not been, he would probably have insisted I went straight to hospital.

I feel so sorry for him. I can't imagine how he must have felt to have me do that in his house. We've always been close; I was best man at his wedding and we'd trained together and even been on the London to Brighton cycle ride together to raise funds to refurbish the gym at Five Star. What must he have thought of me? 'I'm so sorry mate, I said, 'I'm bang out of order. I'm going for a walk.' Before Wayne could stop me, I was out of the door.

It was around 6.30am. Mentally I was shot to bits. I just wanted someone to sit me down and tell me everything would be alright. I decided to go to Matty's. We've known each other since I was 18 when we first met at Top Guard. He was a good man to have at my side when we worked the doors, and he's always been up front with me and would tell me to my face if ever he thought I was in the wrong. That's what I like about him and, to be honest, I've always looked up to him.

Matty would know what to do.

I walked down Princes Avenue in Buckhurst Hill to Matty's place, a distance of about half a mile, and knocked on the door. 'Dom, bloody hell mate, look at you, what a state!'

'I'm in trouble Matty, I really need someone to talk to.'

By now I'd lost quite a bit of blood and Matty was insisting on getting me to the hospital, but I wasn't having it. 'I just need some cotton wool and antiseptic,' I insisted. Matty knew a little about first aid and, in the end, we settled for him bandaging up my wounds. He made a cup of coffee. 'You gotta eat something mate,' he said. We sat down and talked and talked, then he gave me a set of keys and told me to use his house. What a godsend he was when I really needed him.

My head was all over the place. I was thinking it would be best to take up Matty's offer for a while until things calmed down. I was worried the Old Bill would raid Nic's place looking for me. I had vision of the SO19s kicking in the front door; after all, they don't fuck about, and I didn't want to expose Nic or Lauren to anything like that.

Nevertheless, it was only a couple of days later that I went back to Nic's house. That night we went to bed, but I kept my top on, hoping she wouldn't see what I'd done to myself. But she already knew. The local rumour mill had seen to that.

'What have you done?'

'Nothing, I don't want to talk about it.'

How could I put all that had happened on her shoulders? She just cuddled me. Lying next to her I just felt so safe. She just accepts me as I am. Nic isn't silly. She's never bugged me about it since. It's something we've put to bed.

But the next day the paranoia was still there. Unless anyone's been there, they can have no idea of what a devastating effect it can have on you.

By now, Wayne had been in touch with Lenny and Bryn to let them know what had happened. When I visited Bryn at his home in Epping, Lenny turned up too. I'm sure I must have met Bryn for all the right reasons in the first instance because, as long as I can remember, he's always been 100 per cent honest with me – even when I've been wrong. He's one of my best mates because he's never afraid to point out any home truths to my face. But even he and Lenny together could not get through to me and I decided it was time I just got away from it all, somewhere the police wouldn't find me.

It had looked as if I was going to lose everything. In the back of my mind I couldn't help thinking I deserved it all because I'd been such a fucking idiot. Outwardly, I'd been Dom the funny guy but, inside, I'd been cracking up. It was all a front. Nic knew something had been going on, but she didn't know all the details. 'What are you doing to yourself?' she'd ask, but I hadn't wanted to talk about it. Nic reckoned I'd probably hit my lowest point and told me I had to fight back.

I was convinced they were going to nick me and, to tell the truth, the thought of spending the next eight to 15 years inside didn't appeal too much. I decided to piss off to Tenerife to stay with my brother Freddy who was running a bar out there at the time. I'd get myself sorted out, maybe get some bar work, or some work in the building trade, or more door work. I'd be getting away from all my problems. The world would be my oyster, and then Nic could come out and join me with Lauren.

Nic had to put me right. She explained that if I wanted to stay out there, it would probably be the end of us. She'd probably end up coming out to see me, then go back, not see me for a month, and then come back again. She reckoned that, after a time, it would all fizzle out between us. She couldn't bring Lauren out there anyway, away from her Dad. I realised she was right.

I reviewed my situation. The Old Bill would soon find me if I was to stay with Freddy. It wouldn't take them ten minutes to work out where I'd gone. As I had a lot of friends in Tenerife, I decided I'd wait until I got there before finding someone to stay with for a few months and then take it from there.

But first, I'd have to get out of the country undetected by the Old Bill. I worked out a plan of action and asked my mate's mum and dad to help me carry it out. The plan involved driving through France and Spain before catching a flight to Tenerife where Freddy would be waiting for me.

At first the couple tried to dissuade me. They obviously didn't think it was such a good plan but, after much cajoling, they agreed and, eventually, they were happy to help me out. I suggested I should hide in the boot of their car when it came to passing immigration controls.

We left Woodford around 11am. As we approached the harbour at Dover, they stopped the car. I jumped out and, as soon as the coast was clear, I hopped into the boot. I know it sounds a pretty uncomfortable way to travel, but their car was a reasonable size and I wasn't too cramped. In fact, once the car had boarded the ferry, I even managed to sleep for a couple of hours until we arrived in the French port of Calais.

After a while down the road I climbed out of the boot, got back into the car, and we drove southwards through France and into Spain. The journey took 24 hours. We split up in Alicante. From there I flew to Madrid and then caught another plane to Tenerife. Freddy picked me up at the airport. When we met I told him what had been going on. Until that point he'd had no idea and, bearing in mind the gravity of the situation I'd put myself in, he didn't really know what he could say to help me.

We had a drink together at his bar, but I just couldn't settle or sleep at all. A couple of Freddy's mates were telling me how good it was to see me. I decided I wanted to stay in Tenerife but I had so much to sort out and, in the back of my mind, I knew my bail was going to expire in the next 24 hours. Back home, no-one had heard from me in three days. I met up with a couple of friends, Bernie and her husband. I told them I needed to see Bryn and Sarah who were staying at their villa at the time. Bernie took me to meet them.

Bryn's been a bit of a boy in his time, a bit of a face, you might say. But he's changed now. He's married Sarah, and he's gone over to God, which has been a great thing for him. We've been close from the time we first met. I'm sure now, if it hadn't been for him, I'd be dead.

'You've made your bed now, ain't you?' said Bryn as he welcomed me.

'Bryn, I just don't know what I'm doing mate.'

He invited me in and we sat down for a long chat. Bryn and I were so alike years previously when we'd first met, but now he's a saint. He helps so many people.

We sat down together and just talked and talked. 'Look Dom,' he said, 'we can try to sort this out, but you've got to face up to things rather than run away from them.' He pointed out that, if I jumped bail, it would be difficult, maybe impossible, for me to return to Britain in the future – unless I wanted to find myself spending a long time behind bars. He reminded me that my Dad wasn't getting any younger. Who knows, I might not ever be able to see him again. I had to go home he said. That would be the only way to clear up this whole mess.

He spoke so much sense and, even though I'd hit

such a low point, he helped me to get over it. We were both crying and we both had a bit of a pray. 'Please God, help me out here.'

Like Bryn, Sarah has also been a good friend over the years. Although she was aware of all that had been going on, she left Bryn and me to it. Perhaps she thought I would feel more comfortable with a one-to-one chat. Suddenly it actually dawned on me that everything Bryn had been saying seemed to make sense. He gave me a big hug and assured me that he and Sarah would stand by me all the way. 'Listen,' he said, 'we'll fight this with you. Whatever you've done, you've done. We'll help you get over this, but you must learn from it.'

Bryn's phone rang. It was Nick, my solicitor. One of my mates back home had let him know where I was. He'd been trying to help, although I didn't realise it at the time. However, the police had already been in touch with Nick to tell him my bail had been extended for another month.

'He's with me now,' said Bryn.

'You'd better tell him about the bail,' said Nick. 'Things are looking a bit better, else they'd have charged him by now.'

After another long chat with Bryn I picked up the phone. Nic answered.

'Hi Nic, is everything alright?'

'Yes'.

'Good, what are you doing tonight?'

'Nothing.'

'Good, mind if I come round?'

'You bastard, I knew you'd do this!'

We were both crying our eyes out. I remember
flying back into Stansted airport, apprehensive there
could be a repeat of what happened the last time I
touched down there, even though Bryn had already
assured me that, in the eyes of the law, nothing had
been proved that I'd done anything wrong and that I
was still on bail.

That night, as I lay in bed with Nic, I told her that,
maybe, everything was going to be alright after all.
The following day Nic and I went to see her mum
Lorraine and stepdad John. They too tried to reassure
me that everything would, indeed, be okay. In so many
people's eyes I know I'll always be seen as a wrong-un.
How lucky am I to have people around me like Nic,
Lorraine and John?

Look, I'm not a bad person. It's just that I've done
some really bad things. I've got a good heart and I've
got the best of manners – I'm always saying thank you
to people and telling them how much I appreciate this
or that.

I decided I had to cut down on the booze. I wasn't
an alcoholic, but I'd been drinking far too much and,
as a result, I'd been drawing too much attention to
myself. During this time on bail I had been almost
looking for reasons to have a ruck with people. I'd
been so angry, so upset, and thinking why me? Getting
drunk had helped because then I couldn't remember
what the problem was. Sometimes, if I went into a

club, I'd end up on the dance floor laughing hysterically. It's like I couldn't remember I'd been in the frame for an armed kidnapping. I was blanking things out.

All this time, though, the video identification parade had been looming. A week prior to the parade I'd been bailed again. For that I had to go back to Harlow police station to sign in. Trying to sound cheerful I said, 'At least I'll still be out at Christmas.' A copper looked at me stony-faced and said, 'Yeah, but let's make sure it's your last one though, eh?'

Thanks mate.

I got the call. The identification parade was set for the following Wednesday. I went back to Nic. 'I've got something to tell you,' I said.

'I've got something to tell you too. You go first.'

'I've got the ID parade on Wednesday.'

'Yeah, well I'm pregnant.'

'Wicked!' I was absolutely thrilled with the news but that excitement was tempered by the knowledge that the identification parade could have a devastating effect on us both. I was desperately worried.

It wasn't until the Thursday that the call came. I was working out in the gym with some of the lads. Lenny took the call. 'You've not been picked out, you're in the clear.' On top of that, the alleged victim had retracted his statement. They had nothing on me. The gym erupted with cheering. Brilliant!

The news was a huge weight off my shoulders. I suppose the Old Bill hadn't been so bad overall, but they still wanted to talk to me about the smashed up car. One was a policewoman, DCI Brody, and the other was a guy by the name of Anton Roberts. What did I want to do with the car? I told them it wasn't mine, they could do what they liked with it as far as I was concerned.

'Listen,' said Brody, 'Do yourself a favour. Keep out of everyone else's trouble.' Roberts added, 'Just stick to fighting – in the ring, because you're very good at it.' As I came out of Harlow police station I was so relieved it was all over.

Later, I met up with Bryn. 'Dom,' he said, 'You've got a clean slate, now it's up to you to do the right thing.'

Chapter Eight

A HUMBLING EXPERIENCE

The axe attack in the Five Star gym came shortly after I had been cleared of any involvement in the alleged kidnapping. Following the attack I was taken to Oldchurch Hospital in Romford. It was like something you see on the telly hospital drama *ER*. They were all there waiting for me. 'We've got a cerebral haematoma here, blah, blah, blah.' There were about eight of them all working on me at once. 'You've got a bad head injury,' they told me. 'What else have you got?'

I was attached to saline drips and I watched as the bags rapidly emptied into me, they just seemed to suck right in. A nurse examined my right hand and found she was able to put her fingers so far into the axe wound she could see and feel the bones inside. By now

I was naked and a nurse was washing all the blood off me. I had lost around four pints of blood and was very lucky still to be alive. Eventually, they stitched me back together. I had 15 stitches in the back of my head, ten in my left forearm, five in my left hand, and around 20 in my right hand.

It didn't take long for word to get around about what had happened to me. After a while there were around 30 people turning up at the hospital to see how I was. Suddenly, three faces appeared around the door – Matty, Paul and Mark. I nearly shit myself. I'd been convinced these guys had attacked me and I thought they'd come back to finish me off. I know now it was the paranoia – and believe me, you do get a bit jumpy after you've had an axe stuck in your head, but the guys were really upset that I could ever have thought they had anything to do with the attack. It just shows what a bizarre state of mind I'd been in at the time.

Then the Old Bill turned up, wanting to ask more questions. This time they were accompanied by an armed response team which, I gather, is normal procedure if the use of a firearm has been reported in a crime. All told I suppose they were only with me for around five minutes because I wasn't in a particularly helpful frame of mind. As far as I was concerned, what had happened at the gym was nothing to do with anyone else. I told them my injuries had occurred following a burglary at the gym but, of course, they didn't believe that for a moment. They were sure the attack had been linked to the kidnapping investigation. By this time, my mind had been racing, trying to work out who had been responsible for doing me over and now, having eliminated Matty, Paul and Mark from my list of suspects, I reckoned I had a pretty good idea who it was – but there was no way I could ever have told the Old Bill.

My mate Paul and his girlfriend Georgina had contacted Nic to let her know what had happened. They picked her up and brought her to the hospital. When she arrived she was tearful, confused and worried. In fact, I was more worried about her than I was for myself. Then Johnny Fast Hands turned up, and some friends who had interrupted their meal at a restaurant as soon as they'd heard what had happened. Suddenly, I had a much clearer picture of who my real friends were.

A fractured skull was diagnosed. The next day I was taken for an MRI scan. That took the best part of the day and, when that was finished, the National Crime Squad turned up, wanting to interview me. A bloke was asking me what had been going on. Did I know what it was all about? I told him I had no idea. They'd already questioned me the previous evening and told me they had a pretty good idea what had been behind the attack and insisted 'You know too'.

'Do I?'

They told me they didn't want any repercussions. 'We don't want anything happening to anybody. If anything nasty happens, we'll call you right in.' The

Old Bill aren't daft. They knew who I knew. They knew my close friends and associates.

By the time all the medical checks were over I'd got fed up of all the hanging around and was anxious to get out of the place before the Old Bill turned up again and started asking more questions. I decided I didn't want to hang around the hospital a moment longer. 'I want to go home, I want to go home', I kept saying. Despite medical advice to stay at the hospital, I removed all the lines attached to me and discharged myself.

I told Nic I wanted to go to the pub. I needed to be seen out and about. I had a few beers but, if I'd been a little paranoid before the attack, I really was now. I kept thinking they would be coming back to finish me off. But I had to front it out, even though it was fucking scary. Look, I know how these things work. I know how to get to people. It's not as if I'm surrounded by bodyguards. I am who I am, and I don't bow to anyone. I guess that's what fucked me up. I must have said or done the wrong thing to the wrong people.

People are clever, most more than me. See, if I've got the hump with you, you haven't got to wait a couple of years for me to get even. I'd come round and sort you out straight away. People know me for that. If someone wanted to get at me it would be easy to arrange for another person to take the blame because they'd know it wouldn't be long until I upset someone else. Some people are prepared to wait.

I reckon someone just waited a bit longer than most to get at me.

If I was worried about myself, I was even more worried about Nic, after all, she was pregnant at the time. What really upset me was the fact that someone had tried to take away my chance of ever seeing my kid.

From the day I discharged myself I didn't want to go back to any of my old haunts, particularly the gym. However, I did return there a couple of days later. To be honest, it was pretty daunting and I realised the moment I set foot through the door that I wouldn't be training there any more. Lenny was there. I'd told him some time before what my life was all about, but this sequence of events transpired to seriously damage, possibly even ruin, what had been a wonderful relationship between the two of us.

Lenny, and his wife Laurie, had almost been like a substitute mother and father to me for years. I felt so sorry for Lenny – and Wolfie, the young boxer who had called the police during the attack. He's a game kid but, he told me, 'That was too heavy for me'. I wanted to tell Lenny I had to get away. I wanted to take Nic away from it all and go back to Bryn's villa in Tenerife. But, before I could start, Lenny said, 'I want a word.'

I panicked. What had he heard? Were they coming back?

It wasn't that. Lenny became emotional and gave me a hug. 'I'm so sorry mate,' he said. He was really feeling bad that he couldn't have helped me more during the attack. I told him not to be silly and wondered how I could ever have handled the situation if anything had happened to him that night. I'm sure that if he, or Wolfie, had been injured in any way because of me, there's no way I would have been able to forgive myself. As things worked out, I was the only injured party so I could afford to let sleeping dogs lie. I'd learnt my lesson. Don't get me wrong. As long as people don't come near me or my family, I'm alright. I'm not going to go out and start things up.

I felt truly sorry for Lenny. He could have had a heart attack because of me. That's why I decided it would be best for everyone if I kept away from anyone associated with me. That way, perhaps they would be safer. Since then, though, Lenny has taken my sudden lack of contact badly – and I can't say I blame him.

I owe Lenny such a lot – far more than he'll ever know, and I don't care who knows it. He was there for me when I left Gator ABC to go to the Five Star. A trainer from Gator had telephoned Lenny to advise him I was a handful, a bit of a nutter who he shouldn't bother taking on, but Lenny was prepared to spend time on me.

To be honest, I love the geezer. He and Laurie welcomed me into their home as if it was my own. Over the years, a lot of people threw me overboard when things got bad, but Lenny didn't. The least I could have done was to have made the time to sit down with him and to explain properly why I was going to break off and do my own stuff but I did my emu impression and stuck my head in the sand. Later, I went back to Gary Bedford who had been my trainer when I was a 20-year-old at Gator ABC. That must have hurt Lenny terribly.

I could excuse myself by saying that by keeping away from Lenny, they wouldn't come back to the gym looking for me, and that I'd done him a favour by fucking off so Lenny wouldn't have to be involved any more. But that would be just a cop-out really. I should have sat down and talked to him. I should have explained why I had to have a change, that I'd just shut down from everybody. Twice now, I've met Lenny at boxing shows and have tried to shake his hand, but he didn't want it, so I guess it was the last straw.

Although the axe attack in the gym had been a life-threatening experience for me, I have to say, it was not the first time I'd experienced such a serious situation, but that's one of those instances in my life that really cannot go into print for legal reasons.

Nevertheless, after the attack I didn't even want to go back to my flat. I asked a long-standing mate, 'Long-haired' John Froggatt, to pop back to collect my stuff which, in hindsight, was a real liberty.

Meanwhile, in a Clacton hospital, my dad was battling against the cancer that was to eventually claim his life. Dad's death totally devastated me. My world was falling apart.

I usually keep my problems to myself. I remember visiting Mum a couple of weeks after the attack. My hand was still a mess.

'What happened to you?' she asked. 'When did that happen?'

'A couple of weeks ago.'

'You didn't tell me!'

'It's not your problem, Mum.'

Normally, I prefer to sort out my own problems. Although at this particular time in my life I was receiving a good deal of support from my friends, I didn't want my Mum to be worrying about me. After all, what could she have done about anything? That wasn't just for Mum's sake either. With everything else I had to worry about, I didn't need the extra concern of Mum fretting over me.

A couple of weeks after the attack, Nic and I went to Tenerife to stay with Bryn and Sarah in their villa. While there I spent a couple of weeks soul searching and came to the conclusion I'd deserved everything that had happened to me. Back home, despite everything that had happened between us, Lenny had still been covering up for me. He was telling anyone wondering where I was that, because I'd been having such a tough time, what with my old man dying, all the aggro over the kidnapping investigation, and the attack, I'd needed to get away from it all for a while.

Thinking about it, that was one hell of a run of bad luck. I'm glad I didn't win the bloody Lottery at the time because I'd have probably lost the ticket. And, to be honest, I'm glad Dad wasn't aware of the attack in the gym. The shock of it would have probably given him a heart attack and I know he would, at least, have been so upset.

We had a lot of time to think about things in Tenerife. Eventually, everything began to fall into place in my mind. I said to Nic, 'That's it, I'm not going back to all that. I'm going to keep away from my former associates and my old way of life.' When we eventually got home I shut everything down. I changed my telephone number and only kept in touch with a very small circle of trusted people. I didn't want to know anyone any more.

Apart from Nic and the baby, the attack may have been the best thing that's ever happened to me. It put everything into perspective. At the end of the day I have to be thankful no-one else got hurt. God forbid, if they had, there would have been no way I could have let it go. I would have had to find out for sure where all the grief came from. I can sit down now and think of at least 15 or 20 people that might have wanted it done to me, people I've hurt.

Look, I'm a handful. I've done some terrible things, and I know I'm capable of doing similar things again, but it just isn't me any more. I'm not a bully. I was lost. Now I've got this persona about me. People may think they know me but, at the end of the day, I just want to be left alone with my family.

After the attack I needed closure. I knew it only needed one phone call for me to be dragged back into the world I'd been living in, so I decided to start working for Nic's dad on a building site. It's hard work, but it pays the bills and, best of all, it's not dirty money. I guess I'm beginning to learn about responsibility. Looking back to when I was boxing professionally, I remember training first thing in the morning and again at night, but I was always dashing off to see this or that geezer. That's how it was. Now I can concentrate solely on my life without being sidetracked. Nowadays, I'm more focused.

The whole experience of the attack has humbled me. Nic wondered how I could say that. I told her, 'If you had been in what had been my world, seeing how it worked, how you get manipulated, how you get manoeuvred, you'd realise.' I guess I'm not the hardest person to work if you know what buttons to press but, if someone takes just a little time to show me affection, I'd go the whole mile for them. I can't say I was used by certain individuals because I got paid to do each job, to collect money or whatever. Maybe beat people up a little bit.

Nowadays, if money gets a bit tight, there's always the temptation to go out and collect a few debts – the guys who used to pay me to do so would always want me back because of my reputation. However, as soon as I find myself thinking like that I remind myself of how lucky I am to have Nic and the kids, and then I think 'no way'.

Chapter Nine

THE FOUR-
CORNERED RING

Of course, I'm best known as a boxer and, I like to think, a bloody good one. Over the years I've won a succession of titles in both amateur, professional and unlicensed contests, and it's been a profession that has given me huge satisfaction.

When I started working at Leytonstone in my teens, I would go to the nearby Hyams gym. I suppose that's where my real involvement in the sport began, although I'd had a taste of what was involved six years earlier when Dad took me to Gator ABC.

Hyams was a terrific gym with a terrific atmosphere. I really enjoyed going there. Although it was a bodybuilding and fitness gym there was also a boxing ring and a couple of punchbags, and you could spar with anyone who turned up. It was at Hyams where I first met Bobby Wilcox who became a good friend to me, as did a chap called Clive who was the head doorman at Charlie Chang's nightclub near the Walthamstow dog track.

I learned a lot from Bobby and Clive. Bobby, although he was, shall we say, a big man – maybe a little over his fighting weight – sure knew how to handle himself, while Clive was only a little fella but you should never judge a book by its cover – he was a tough, tough man, lethal almost. In fact, when Clive and I began training together he taught me a lot about boxing.

I spent a lot of time sparring at Hyams. As long as you had a gumshield you could go in the ring with whoever you liked. That's the way it was. I often sparred with really good kids, including some who had already boxed as amateurs. The idea was to learn the techniques, not necessarily to bash each other up. I'd spar with anybody who turned up. It didn't matter to me how big they were. That's how it was. That's how you learn.

I soon acquired the nickname 'Slugger' because they reckoned I didn't know any other way to fight other than going right in at full steam ahead. However, after a while, they taught me to slow down a little and to pick my shots. I'm sure that if it hadn't been for Bobby and Clive – and Gary Bedford who later trained me as an amateur – I wouldn't have had such a good start in the game when I began boxing as an amateur.

Compared to most of the guys at the gym, I suppose

I was just a kid, but I never turned down an invitation to spar. I loved it. It gave me the opportunity to learn about discipline in the ring and taught me to defend myself at all times. In fact, I spent so much time sparring before I ever actually boxed.

Mind you, I saw some people smashed to bits while sparring, some even knocked spark out – particularly if they'd got into the ring to spar with someone they hardly knew. Trouble is, you're always going to get some guys who don't really want to spar – they're just looking for an opportunity to show what they can do. To beat someone up. A boxing ring, I found out very early on, can be a hard place to be.

Some people got into the ring and just took liberties, knocking people out. Then it would be a bucket of cold water over them to bring them round again. No doubt about it, if you thought you were better than you really were, this was the place where you'd soon be brought back down to earth.

I sustained a few good hidings there myself, but I still came back for more. Once, Bobby was training a few of us on the pads. There was me, a chap called Darren from Chingford, another called Ed, and another called Mike who, if I remember rightly, was a double ABA champion. In fact, Mike was never one to take liberties and he was a brilliant guy to train with.

After a while we began sparring with each other but, within a few minutes, another guy strolled into the gym. He had all the gear – the cup, the guard, the gumshield, the lot. He came up to me and asked if I fancied sparring with him. 'Yeah, course I will,' I replied enthusiastically, even though I didn't know the guy from Adam. If I had known he was a professional boxer I might have considered his offer a lot more carefully but, me being me, I just saw it as another opportunity to spar with someone new.

By the time we'd spent a few moments together in the ring I hardly knew what had been hitting me. He was taking me to pieces. But I wouldn't give in. I just kept going. I'd been taught how to double cover, backing into the ropes with both my hands up to take all the shots before throwing punches back, but he was really unloading the punches against me. Daft thing was, though, I was actually enjoying it. Well, at least until he started getting sarcastic with me.

'What's the matter, mate?' he said. 'The lights are on but nobody's at home!'

'What do you mean by that?' I replied.

'Well, you're getting hit all the time.'

'So? You're not hurtin' me.'

He was a flash bastard. I remember Darren, who was about five years older than me, saying to him, 'Hold on mate, this is only meant to be sparring – we ain't here to bash each other up!'

The following night we were back in the gym. While working on the pads I noticed Bobby and Darren talking to each other. Then I noticed Flash Bastard had returned. Again, he came up to me and asked if I wanted to spar with him.

'Sure,' I said.

As I was getting ready, Bobby and Darren walked up to Flash Bastard. Bobby asked him if he fancied sparring with him.

'Yeah, okay, but I'll spar with him first,' said Flash Bastard, nodding towards me.

'No mate,' said Bobby. 'Spar with *me* first. Dominic can have a go afterwards. Anyway, I'm a bit rusty.'

Flash Bastard got kitted up and stepped into the ring with Bobby. Bobby started moving around and throwing jabs. Then Flash Bastard tried showboating by swinging a huge right hook but Bobby was instinctively quick enough to roll under it and delivered a beautiful left hook to the body which promptly dropped Flash Bastard onto the canvas, rolling around in agony.

'Are you alright mate?' asked Bobby as if he was concerned. 'Breathe in, breathe in, it won't hurt so much.'

At this point I realised that Bobby was actually taking the piss out of him.

'I'm alright, I'll be okay,' wheezed Flash Bastard.

Bobby waited for him to get back to his feet and they continued sparring. Then Bobby done him again, this time with a beauty on the chin just as Flash Bastard was about to throw a left hook. Instead, he went crashing down onto the canvas and ended up sitting on his arse.

'I think that'll do for now,' said Bobby nonchalantly.

Flash Bastard wasn't looking too comfortable.

'What's the matter, mate?' asked Bobby. 'I guess you

don't like people taking liberties, do you? Well, let me tell you – we don't like it either!'

Darren took me to one side. 'We saw what he was doing to you last night,' he said, 'and we didn't like it.' I told Darren I hadn't minded. 'Maybe not, but we do. It ain't meant to be like that here.'

Then Bobby called me into the ring, as if to show Flash Bastard what it was all about. He guided me through the session: 'That's it son, use the jab, come on, use your jab, that's it, well done.'

Bobby had certainly taught Flash Bastard a lesson. It had been so cool the way he'd taken him out. I remember as I'd watched them in action. Although Bobby was not at his physical finest, and Flash Bastard looked as fit as you like, it was BANG, BANG, BANG, all over. Bobby had made it look so easy.

'Fuckin' hell,' I thought. 'I wish I could do that!'

Bobby and Darren taught me so much. They worked so hard to help me improve my skills because at this time I still wasn't a boxer. I was a gym fighter and there's a big difference between the two. Every time I got into the ring I didn't really want to jab and move. My instincts made me want to just go straight for it and to smash 'em up. That's why they had to work so hard to instil the basic art of boxing in me.

After a while, Bobby told me I was a good gym fighter but I was wasted at Hyams and that I should get myself in at a proper club to get some fights under my belt so I joined Gator ABC. Johnny Kingsley became my new trainer but, because he had his professional licence, he wasn't allowed to do the corner work so, for my first amateur contest, Lenny was in my corner.

I was about 20 years old at the time. The fight was at Tilbury Working Men's Club, on a Belhus Park show, although I can't remember the name of the lad I fought. It was three two-minute rounds, and we had a proper ding-dong. I was cheered on by Mum and Dad and around 30 friends.

Prior to the fight I'd been sparring with a professional called Darren Westover which was pretty useful to me that night. The kid I was due to fight had been trying to psyche me out at the pre-fight medical. He got on the scales and started taking the piss out of me and pointing to the black eye Darren had given me earlier and reckoned I'd have another one before he'd finished with me. I weighed in at about 86 kilos, around 13 and a half stone.

I couldn't be serious to save my life at the time. I was always walking around with a silly grin on my face, laughing and joking. Lenny had already been told I was a bit 'different' but I don't think he could have imagined quite how much. Lenny got hold of me. 'Listen, do you realise this is serious?'

'Yeah, yeah, don't worry about it.'

Even so, I have to admit to a few nerves leading up to the fight, any fighter feels that to some extent but, in the first round, I went out and got him with a big jab and blood came pissing out of his nose. After that, we just locked horns for two minutes, knocking the shit out of each other. It was mad. At the bell, Lenny gave me a slap. 'What do you think you're doing? I want you to *box* this geezer! I want to see you hit him with a jab, off the jab and right hand, straight shot!' After that it was easy and I got a unanimous points decision. I really smashed him up. Trouble is, I just can't resist a tear-up and that, over the years, was one of Lenny's biggest problems with me.

I'd won my first contest and had taken the first step towards a dream – to become a professional boxer. At this stage, however, my training programme was nothing like I would require to make the grade as a professional in later years. Training was limited to working the pads and sparring, but I wasn't doing any running or much else at all. I always believed I was a great fighter but, I have to admit, I had to work and train hard over the years before I became a good boxer. I particularly had to work long and hard to perfect my jab and my counter-punching – techniques I did not fully acquire until a considerable time later.

As an amateur I fought in the Port of London Authority's finals for which I had to get down to 12 stone 7 pounds. I boxed a kid called Michael Osenburt, a black kid from Walthamstow, a really nice bloke. I was warned I'd have to watch him because he was such a banger. So it proved. I got him with a good jab in the first round but the next thing I knew I was sitting on my arse, courtesy of a terrific right hook. Because I'd been sparring with the professionals I'd learnt a trick or two. I jumped up and leant against the ropes so Michael could wear himself out before I would concentrate on getting back at him. Trouble was, they don't like that sort of thing in the amateur game. Michael came at me full on and the referee stepped in and stopped the fight. 'What did you do that for?' I asked. He told me he could see I wasn't hurt but, as I wasn't throwing any punches back, he had to stop the contest. One of life's lessons, I guess.

I lost my last fight at Gator ABC against a lad called Adrian Tooze from Swaffham – a daylight robbery at the Prince Regent Hotel at Woodford Bridge.

I decided to join Lenny at the Five Star ABC at Harold Hill. By now I was 21 years old. My first fight for Five Star was at the Brewsters Hall in Romford. Earlier I'd asked Lenny a favour. I wanted Adrian Tooze. Lo and behold, I got him and this time he didn't know what hit him. I smashed him up. A while later I was in against Tooze again, this time at Swaffham on their show. I beat him again.

But boxing wasn't my only interest in contact sport. I'd always been interested in karate. From the age of 16 I'd competed in the sport and actually went on to do pretty well at it. I remember my first fight as a white belt. I was competing in the open *kumite*, where you can fight anybody, at a competition in Colchester. I had my pads on and cracked this kid on the nose, making it bleed, and promptly got myself disqualified. It didn't put me off the sport though, as I eventually worked my way up to become a black belt in Shotokan karate while training at a club in Woodford.

Later, I was living in the Cambridge area with one of Freddy's friends. I'd gone up there looking for some door work but couldn't find much so I moved further north to a place just outside Darlington where I remained for around eight months. While I was there I got into Muay-Thai boxing. It's like boxing, but it's a lot harder because you're allowed to use your elbows and knees. It's full contact.

However, I couldn't find many opportunities for door work up north so I returned to Essex and picked up my boxing again. In 1994, I beat a lad called Stevie Lucas from West Ham in the North East Divisionals. I stopped him in the third round. Then I lost in the London ABAs against Vic Clarke. This was followed by a fight against Wayne Gibson who had earlier beaten Danny Williams in the ABAs. The following year I had just two fights, the first against Stevie Lucas again – I stopped him again in the third round – and a Repton ABC lad called Everton Crawford who I really bashed up.

A knee injury forced me out of the London ABAs so it was not until the next year that I fought a kid called Marcus Lee, from Repton ABC, who beat me on a majority decision. I went for revenge at The Country Club in Epping Forest, and the bugger done me on another majority decision.

I decided my up and down results needed to improve. I needed consistency. I decided to start training properly and to take my boxing a lot more seriously.

Who knows, I could even turn professional. After all, I was now 26 years old, and selling a lot of tickets.

My last amateur fight was at the Working Men's Club in Romford. Marcus Lee again. He was giving it all that, reckoning he could knock me out this time, but I smashed him to bits in two rounds. I remember the first round. Blatant as ever, I got in close and connected with his forearm, knocking it into his face. 'Oi! any more of that and you're out of here,' said the ref. 'Bloody hell Dom, you can't get away with that,' said Lenny as I went back to my corner at the bell.

I grinned. 'I just did, didn't I?'

But Lenny was adamant, insisting that all he wanted me to do was to use my jab. I did, and got him with a beauty. He went all wobbly, then, for good measure, I split his lip wide open and the ref stopped the fight.

I had already spoken casually to Matchroom Boxing promoter Barry Hearn when I met him at a boxing event about the possibility of signing up with him at some stage, but before Barry and I had got around to meeting up to discuss it in his office, Lenny took me to see promoter Mickey Duff. Mickey offered me £600 per fight, which I thought was crap money. Mickey told us to go away and to think about it. Eventually, Lenny and I thought we'd go along with it so we went back to see Mickey. This time he told us he'd spoken to a couple of people who reckoned I should spend another year as an amateur. I just thought he was trying to get the money down. 'Thanks a lot Mickey. Your loss, not mine!'

Afterwards we went to see Frank Maloney, another top promoter who, among others, had Lennox Lewis on his books. 'I thought you'd have come to see me earlier than this,' he said. Frank's PR man Ed Robinson, himself a pretty good former boxer, filled Frank in and he agreed to a deal. £1,200 for my first fight, plus 10 per cent of my ticket sales. That's more like it! I have to say that, for all the years Frank promoted me he looked after me really well and never took a penny off me.

And so it was 'The Milky Bar Kid' turned professional. The nickname was a long-standing one that I was happy to adopt. I didn't want a moniker such as 'The Terminator' or something of that ilk. The Milky Bar Kid chocolate advertisements on the telly many years previously had featured a lad who, according to many of my friends, was the spitting image of me. They gave me the nickname and it just stuck throughout my boxing career.

As a fledgling professional, an even more punishing training regime suddenly came into force, although of course, training is only one aspect of fitness and healthy living for anyone looking to take up boxing as a career. Diet is also important. Every day, except Thursdays and Sundays, I would begin the day with a bowl of porridge oats made with boiling water prior to my 6am run. It was horrible – tasting rather like wallpaper paste. Then, every couple of hours, I'd have a small portion of rice with chicken, or tuna with half a baked potato – and I'd never eat after 7pm. I didn't drink alcohol, apart from a couple of glasses of wine, topped up with lemonade, on a Friday evening. Even on my days off I would still eat sensibly, and I'd still go to the gym then, afterwards, I'd treat myself to a nice bowl of pasta.

Professional sportsmen and women can only get as much out of their sport as they are prepared to put into it, which is why I took my training so seriously. But some rules are much harder to adhere to than others.

Sex for instance.

It is widely believed a sportsperson should abstain from sexual activity prior to a contest or game in order to preserve their energy. At first, that wasn't too much of a problem for me. Although at the time I had a long-term girlfriend, she would always move out of our flat a couple of weeks before a contest so I could fully concentrate on preparing myself.

After that relationship ended, I used to prefer to be on my own for a couple of nights before a fight anyway, so it was never an issue and, towards the end of my professional career, I wasn't really with anyone in a serious enough relationship. It was only in the later stages of my career – when Nic and I moved in together – that, sometimes, the urge just could not be resisted. But, what the hell!

Long-haired John and I had a tradition when I was boxing. The night before a fight I would always stay at John and his girlfriend Caroline's home in Manor Park. We'd sit up half the night sharing a drink and chatting. Usually, he would have picked me up after the weigh-in and we'd all chill out together, listening to

John's favourite Red Indian music or Phil Collins CDs. Then I'd kip on his couch.

John emits such a calming influence, which is perfect if you've got to fight the following day. I've known him for around 12 years now. He's a good man and has a couple of kids of his own. He's so chilled out – even when I'm fuming about something. When I've got the hump I can even scare myself, but John doesn't let it get to him at all. It's usually, 'Come on Dom, let's go for a walk' or 'Come on Dom, let's have a drink', otherwise he'll make me answer my own questions.

'Why's this then, John?' or 'it's a liberty John, why's that?'

'Dunno Dom, *you* tell *me* why.'

The routine of regular training could seem rather boring to some people but there are ways to vary a fitness regime. Cycling for instance. My training partner and pal Wayne Cummings and I entered the London to Brighton cycle ride one year. It was a beautifully sunny day when we arrived at the starting line in London's Blackheath where the thousands of entrants were cheered on by thousands more onlookers. If I remember correctly, the distance to be covered was around 57 miles but Wayne and I decided that, because of our regular running and gym exercises, there would be no need to take on any other exercises for this event though, looking back, it might have been wiser if we had. I know we ended the day feeling pretty saddlesore!

As I didn't possess a bike of my own, a good friend,

Neil Harriott, who, ironically, just happens to be very well up in the police force, lent me his Diamondback mountain bike. And so it was Wayne and I set off from the starting line, accompanied by a host of entrants who were either just going along for the ride, or raising money for charities. There was also a collection of guys dressed as women, possibly because they thought it would be a fun to go in fancy dress, or possibly not. Who knows?

When we got to what we thought was the halfway mark, Wayne and I called in at a pub for a swift pint of Guinness, then continued on our way. Just over four hours from leaving Blackheath, the coast at Brighton came into sight. Before the ride Wayne and I had agreed we would cross the finishing line side by side but, when we arrived on the seafront, we happened to glance at each other and just knew that wasn't going to happen. Our competitive nature no doubt.

Wayne is a real powerhouse and, as we sped up, he began to overtake me. Just as he was passing me a woman stepped out in front of him. Wayne had to brake really hard to avoid crashing into her which gave me the opportunity to nip in front of him and cross the line just seconds before him.

Obviously, my training involved a lot of road running, so it seemed logical to enter the London Marathon. It was something I'd always fancied having a go at so, in 2000, I lined up at the start, accompanied by Bryn who, earlier that day, had arrived from Tenerife and had not had a wink of sleep – hardly good preparation for such a strenuous event, but you wouldn't have thought so by the way he ran. I remember running along The Embankment when a little git gave me a swift kick up the arse as he passed me. Although he had his back to me, I recognised boxer Spencer Oliver's ears straight away. 'Oi you little bugger!' I called out. He turned around and grinned broadly at me. A few paces further I was aware of a guy hanging from a lamppost. 'Keep goin' Dom!' Boxer Mark Delaney was cheering me on.

I finished the 26.2 miles in 4 hours 4 minutes (which, I'm told, is around an hour and a half quicker than former world heavyweight champion Frank Bruno got around the course that day), while Bryn, despite suffering from really bad cramps, followed me in just 25 minutes later. It was a really emotional day for the both of us, and it's certainly something I'd like to do again sometime.

Tennis is another form of exercise that I've found to be enjoyable. A good friend of mine reckons I could be a really good player because I hit the ball so hard. Trouble is, I just can't control where it goes!

Chapter Ten

NIGHTMARES IN THE RING

The vast majority of my professional career was fought in the cruiserweight division. My first professional fight was in September 1996. I beat Gareth Thomas at York Hall, Bethnal Green in the second round after putting him down in the first.

It was great to get my professional career off to a winning start, particularly as I'd made my debut in one of the traditional homes of British boxing, in the heart of London's East End, just a stone's throw from the hospital where I'd been born 26 years earlier.

The venue has staged so many contests in the past, showcasing the talents of a who's who in boxing, including the likes of Charlie Magri, Lennox Lewis, Joe Bugner and Chris Eubank. The atmosphere there is always electric. In fact, former world welterweight champion John H Stracey once said, 'You had to put on a show at York Hall because the crowd were right on top of you. You could hear everything they said. I remember this one guy giving me so much stick, when I turned round to go back to my corner I thought he'd be sitting on my stool.'

Bethnal Green is steeped in boxing history, so it is hardly surprising so many young men from the area fancy making their marks in the four-cornered ring. The area is blessed for young talent, not least from the nearby Repton Amateur Boxing Club. In fact, Daniel Mendoza, who lived in Paradise Row, Bethnal Green for 30 years, was the champion of England from 1792 to 1795.

Boxing seems to attract spectators of, shall we say, a dubious nature, although, once you get to know some of them, they turn out to be really nice fellas. York Hall, being in London's East End, is situated in what was the heartland of Ronnie and Reggie Kray's gangland empire so it's not surprising that some of their former associates or other former villains sometimes turn up at shows there. That's not to say they're villains now though, it's just that they used to do different things for a living to most other men living in mainstream society. I've met 'Mad' Frankie Fraser a few times. He's spent more than 40 years behind bars, thanks to his sidelines as a former partner in crime to racehorse swindlers and train robbers. Formerly an associate of Charlie Kray, Frankie eventually joined the infamous rival Richardson brothers and, allegedly, had a penchant for inflicting pain.

I've also met Freddie Foreman at various boxing shows. He's a former Kray henchman who's become widely known as the Managing Director of British Crime. Foreman had his own gang in the 1960s which received the body of East End hardman Jack the Hat McVitie following his murder in 1967 at a London basement flat. McVitie had apparently welched on a contract killing so Ronnie Kray had pointed a gun to his head but, when it jammed, brother Reggie repeatedly stabbed McVitie to death with a knife. Foreman once admitted to the murder of two gangland rivals and, although now he is going straight, he became one of the most infamous former villains in the East End of London.

Joe Pyle Junior is another man with a chequered past. Now a boxing promoter, Joe had gangland connections a few years ago. That's all behind him now though. Joe and I occasionally went for drinks together at the Thursday Club near London's Old Kent Road. Another Kray associate, the late Tony Lambrianou, was often there with Joe.

Tony and his brother Chris, who were both in their twenties in 1967, were imprisoned for 15 years for their part in Jack McVitie's murder. Tony was proper old school. That's just the way he was. He served his time inside, but he kept his mouth shut – and you don't get too many like that these days. Compared to these guys, some of the people I've found myself associated with in the past are just dogs.

After I'd beaten Thomas, Frank Maloney asked me

if I fancied another fight within the next couple of weeks. And so it was I fought Pat Lawrence at the Broadway Theatre in Barking and knocked him spark out in the second round.

Next up was Naveed Anwar at York Hall, Bethnal Green. He came at me like a loon in the first round until I started landing on him with every shot – boom, boom, boom. In the second round I connected with a left hook, then a right hook which had him spinning in the air, and then I just smashed him. He pulled out prior to the third round.

My next two fights were both against a really nice fella – Nigel Rafferty, the first at the Elephant and Castle Recreation Centre in Southwark, the second in Enfield on Spencer Oliver's undercard at the Lee Valley Leisure Centre, Picketts Lock. I won each contest on points.

My next contest was my first opportunity to win a professional title, against Southern Area champion Chris Henry from Tottenham at the Grundy Park Leisure Centre in Cheshunt. I'd always had a good following ever since my amateur days but, on this particular evening as I approached the ring, the place erupted with cheers and I suddenly realised what terrific support I really had.

It was 17 June 1997, a date that will be etched on my mind for two reasons, but they couldn't be more diverse. Up to this point in my professional career I'd only had four round contests. Should it go all the way, this would be a ten-rounder. I'd seen Chris box as an amateur so I knew he was very good, even though he'd had a rather shaky start to his professional career. He lost his first fight, being knocked out by Chris Okoh in the second round if I remember correctly. After that, Chris won a couple of fights then took a break. He lost his comeback fight, then embarked on a good run, beating Paul Douglas and Darren Westover for the Southern Area title along the way.

I trained really hard for this fight, and what a cracker it turned out to be. It was the first time I'd ever gone ten rounds and we were toe-to-toe all the way. This was one of the hardest fights I've ever been involved in, really physical, as Chris certainly had a lot of heart. I remember Lenny telling me at the start of the last round that I had to knock him out because I was behind on points. Frank Maloney was telling me I had to be prepared to die out there if I wanted to get my hands on that title.

In sparring, I'd been working on a particular shot for ages. It involved rolling under the right hand as I threw the jab, and coming back with a banger. I was really knackered by now, but it just happened perfectly. I caught Chris with the right hook and followed up with about five more as he sagged against the ropes. It was all over. I was the Southern Area champion but, because of what happened next, there would be no celebrations that night.

I was feeling pretty pleased with myself in my corner. Lenny was congratulating me and I was waiting to be presented with the Southern Area belt when, suddenly, Chris keeled over onto the canvas. I could tell straight away that something was seriously wrong with him and, immediately, the medics jumped into the ring. But Chris just laid there motionless.

'We'd better watch this, Dom,' said Lenny. 'I think he's hurt.'

'Oh shit!'

I could see they were struggling to save his life and, to tell the truth, I was absolutely terrified. I was sure he was going to die right there in the ring. It was a terrible scene that faced everyone concerned, myself, Lenny, Chris's cornermen, the crowd, and millions of Eurosport television viewers – the fight had been screened live. After what seemed like an eternity, Chris was stretchered out to a waiting ambulance and rushed to Oldchurch Hospital in Romford where a blood clot to the brain was diagnosed. His life was in serious danger.

As soon as the ambulance left with Chris, the remainder of the bill was cancelled, which was just as well as I'm sure no-one still had an appetite for more boxing. One top promoter, who shall remain nameless, came over and told me, 'You'd better expect the worst. Pray for him Dom 'cos it don't look that good.' My fears for Chris were alleviated somewhat when I was informed that he had regained consciousness and was sitting up in his hospital bed but, in fact, nothing could have been further from the truth. And so it was that my first professional title win turned out to be a huge and tragic anti-climax. I got showered and dressed then went out for a drink and a pizza. I was back in the gym the next day, but all I could think about was Chris. At the end of the day though, the way I had to look at it was that we were both over 21, and no-one had forced us to climb into a ring together.

Obviously, it was in all the newspapers and the television and radio news. I was still pretty battered from the fight and so upset for Chris and, of course, for his family and friends. Then two idiots walked in. One of them saw my bruises and quipped: 'Cor, you look as bad as the bloke they took to hospital after the boxing last night!' My mate told him to shut his gob: 'That's the bloke who put him there,' he explained. 'Oh fuck, sorry mate.'

I received a telephone call from Frank Maloney. He told me that everyone was worried about me and, although I'd shown I'd been a real warrior in the ring, if I was worried about anything at all, I should go and see him. Frank added that he'd heard I was sporting a couple of black eyes and suggested I wore dark glasses to hide them. I declined his advice. As far as I was concerned I was proud of them. They were my battle scars after a hard, hard fight. I wasn't ashamed of them.

Frank advised me it might be a good idea not to answer my phone for a while because the press were clamouring for comments. I knew that was true – and Lenny had received a few calls too. Basically, Lenny had told everyone that I was too upset over what had happened to Chris and that I didn't want to talk to anyone about it.

Soon afterwards, I made my way to the hospital to see how Chris was doing. In fact, I went twice but, each time, I couldn't find it in myself to actually walk through the door. I imagined how his family must have been feeling. How would they react if the bloke responsible for putting Chris in that state was to walk into the same room? I never did see him, though, from what I understand, thank God, he did pull through.

I decided it would be best for me if I was to go away for a while to convalesce. Even in training I'd only ever sparred for six rounds and there's such a lot of difference between six rounds in the gym and ten rounds in a competitive title fight – particularly against someone like Chris – a very good fighter.

I remember that, as we'd gone into the latter stages of the contest, I'd been thinking to myself that I could beat Chris, that the only person who could ever beat me was myself. I still believe that to this day.

Obviously, what happened to Chris reignited the calls for boxing to be banned.

Boxing correspondent Ivan Sage, who regularly attended my contests, was ringside when Chris collapsed. This is how he reported what happened and how he defended the sport:

Without doubt, this is the most difficult report I have had to write since I have been covering boxing for this newspaper. I refer of course to the events that unfolded before me at the Grundy Park Leisure Centre in Cheshunt on Tuesday evening when the proceedings were brought to a premature end following a terrible injury sustained by Tottenham's Chris Henry.

Henry had just taken part in a 10 round Southern Area cruiserweight title contest with Havering's Dominic Negus and, as Negus celebrated a final round knockout victory, Henry collapsed back onto the canvas. The resultant scenes will never be forgotten by those present as paramedics and a ringside doctor fought desperately to save Henry's life.

Standing ringside to photograph and report on the evening's contests, I witnessed, at close quarters, boxing's ultimate nightmare, and what I saw left me with a feeling of total helplessness and deep concern as those attending the stricken boxer exchanged angry words with each other as they frantically worked to insert an airway to assist Henry's breathing.

After what seemed an eternity, although it was probably just over 10 minutes, Henry was transferred by ambulance to Oldchurch Hospital in Romford where, upon his arrival, he underwent emergency neuro-surgery.

As a result of the ambulance taking Henry to hospital there was no back-up ambulance cover at the venue after the accident, so it was not possible to recommence the proceedings and the rest of the evening's six bouts – including Basildon boxer Georgie Smith's Southern Area title contest and

*Hornchurch middleweight Jason Ratcliff's fight –
were cancelled.*

*The audience, who had waited patiently,
reacted admirably to the announcement. The
events they had witnessed had put everything into
perspective and, to be honest, if they felt the same
way as me, they would have had little appetite for
any further action.*

*No doubt, the events of Tuesday evening will
fuel the anti-boxing debate and, it has to be said,
the people who want to see the sport banned may
have some valid points to make.*

*Boxing has to be seen to get its house in order,
particularly with regard to the prompt availability
of a structured medical response to such a
situation and the close proximity of a suitable
neuro-surgical unit.*

*However, I have been fortunate enough to witness
at first hand some marvellous boxing moments
while covering the sport for this newspaper, not least
Frank Bruno's world championship win at Wembley
Stadium, and I have got to know several boxers –
especially those who train at Barry Hearn's
Matchroom gymnasium in Romford.*

*Each and every one of them is more than aware
of the dangers associated with their sport. Like
any contact sport, boxing has its risks. But to
suggest the sport be banned would, I believe, be a
retrograde step. It could force the sport
underground and, while I wholly accepted that*

may not be considered to be a convincing argument to legitimise the sport, it should also be noted that the attributes required to succeed to the highest level are discipline and self control.

Boxing offers many young men the opportunity to make something of their lives, a sense of purpose and, in the process, the potential to earn a decent living.

As Matchroom trainer Freddie King never tires of telling anyone willing to listen, 'Boxing gives youngsters a sense of discipline and keeps them out of trouble. It provides a controlled channel for their natural aggression.'

I happen to agree with him totally.

It may seem rather trite to do so, but I would be doing Dominic Negus and Chris Henry a disservice not to mention a few details of their contest. In a nutshell, Henry, the Southern Area champion, and Negus, in only his sixth professional contest, both turned in a thrilling non-stop display of boxing for nine rounds, keeping the audience spellbound as they defied their tiredness to exchange punches at an incredible pace.

In between each round both men acknowledged the efforts of their opponent with a smile and the entire contest was fought in a magnificent spirit – both men a credit to their profession.

As they entered the tenth and final round, Henry came out guns blazing and Negus responded accordingly. With just under two minutes of the round gone, Negus delivered a combination to send Henry down and referee Tony Walker had no hesitation in stepping in to end the contest. A delighted Negus embraced his trainer Lenny Butcher but, out of their line of view, Henry was in big trouble on the canvas – a tragic end to a magnificent contest.

At the time of going to press, Henry was reported to be in a 'critical but stable condition' following neuro-surgery.

The thoughts and prayers of all boxers and fans will undoubtedly be with Chris Henry and his family at this traumatic time.

The following week, as the clamour to ban boxing increased, Ivan wrote the following article:

Following the tragic injuries sustained by Tottenham boxer Chris Henry last week after his contest with Essex boxer Dominic Negus, the British Medical Association (BMA) – and many others – have called once again for the sport to be banned. Yet again the anti-boxing lobby has been given strong evidence to back up their argument that this sport has no place in a civilised society.

The sight of Chris Henry lying on the canvas as medics battled to save his life at the end of his contest will haunt many of us who were present that night.

Moments earlier, Henry and Negus had served

up a fantastic contest, which had delighted the audience over its previous 10 action-packed rounds. Then there was stunned silence.

At ringside, I witnessed scenes that made me question my love of the sport. I did not know Henry personally, but my heart ached for him just to open his eyes to reassure everyone he was going to be alright.

I have many friends who box. How would I have felt if it had been one of them lying there in front of me?

Too many times boxing fans have been called upon to question their consciences. Is it really a blood-lust that we wish to satisfy? At times like this, it would be easy to adopt a knee-jerk response, jump on the bandwagon and call for a total ban on the sport, but is it really the answer?

I respect the opinions of the BMA. I would not wish to trivialise their arguments – after all, the doctors are the ones left to pick up the pieces every time a boxer is injured. One ring death or serious injury is one too many and it is natural, and right, that every incident should cause great concern.

I often make an analogy to horse racing – a sport I believe to be cruel. I know many people will dispute this view but, to see a racehorse ridden around a course with a rider on its back, over fences, to the point of exhaustion, for the satisfaction and reward of its owner, rider and racegoers, is something I find hard to justify.

A racehorse that falls and breaks a leg will most likely be shot – something that happens frequently each year at racecourses all over the country as it is no longer a viable, money-making proposition. Where is the public outcry whenever this occurs?

Boxers are able to make an informed choice whether or not to partake in their sport. A racehorse has no such choice.

At the time of going to press, a spokeswoman at Romford's Oldchurch Hospital described boxer Chris Henry's condition as 'stable but poorly' after undergoing surgery to remove a blood clot from his brain.

A few days later I met Ivan at a boxing bill at York Hall. We had a chat and, a few days later, he wrote:

It was good to see Havering-atte-Bower boxer Dominic Negus ringside at Bethnal Green on Monday evening. Making his first public appearance since his Southern Area cruiserweight victory over Chris Henry, Negus had been keeping out of the media spotlight after the events following the contest when Henry was critically injured in the ring.

'After the fight, I had to get away for a while to get my thoughts together,' said Dominic. 'I have been so upset by what happened to Chris, it's all been a lot to take in.

'Tonight I watched Basildon boxer Georgie

Smith win the Southern Area light welterweight belt and I couldn't help thinking how I wished I could have enjoyed my moment of glory as much as he did.

'Winning the Southern Area championship should have been a wonderful moment for me, but no belt is worth a boxer being badly injured. Thank God, I've been told the hospital believe it's possible Chris may make a full recovery, but I can't let what happened to Chris affect my boxing – after all, boxing is all I have, and I'm a very hungry fighter.'

The debate raged on. In fact, the sport will always be contentious, simply because of its nature – aiming to defend yourself at all times while trying to stop the guy opposite you by hitting him around the body and head as hard and as often as you are able. Thankfully, incidents like what happened to Chris are rare but, in May 1998, my nightmare was relived. Promoter Jess Harding had given me tickets to watch my mate Spencer Oliver's European title contest against Sergei Devakov at London's Royal Albert Hall. Spencer and I had boxed together several times on the amateur circuit and also on professional shows. Against Devakov, Spencer was put down in the first round but had got up and performed well until Devakov put him down again in the tenth. Spencer beat the count but the referee stopped the fight anyway. Then Spencer collapsed.

Just like Chris Henry.

For me, it was a bad, bad dream. Don't get me wrong. Even today, I'm gutted about what happened to Chris – I still think about him and his family a lot – but, when it happened to Spencer, I couldn't believe it. It hadn't been so long previously that I'd witnessed medics frantically working on Chris, and now they were doing the same with Spencer.

Just before Spencer collapsed, I'd been chatting ringside to former boxer Charlie Magri. Lenny had been sitting just in front of us in the ringside VIP seats. He came over to me.

'Come on Dom,' he said, 'I'm getting you out of here – you don't need to be seeing this.'

Later that week, Ivan filed the following report:

It was a scene I had been hoping against hope I would never witness again as, just four or five feet in front of me, Spencer Oliver lay prone on the canvas as medics desperately struggled to save his life.

Just half an hour earlier, Spencer had entered the arena to all the razzmattaz that accompanies most of the big fights nowadays – smoke, music and, to top it all, a full choir as he spectacularly rose into view on a platform from behind the choir. In the ring, Sergei Devakov waited patiently as his opponent made his entrance.

I am not even going to attempt to report on

174

what happened over the following 10 rounds of action, save for mentioning that Spencer was floored in the first round, but rose to give Devakov plenty to think about for the next nine.

But, during the tenth round, a punch put Spencer down and, although he beat the count, the referee put his arms around him to steady him and halted the proceedings. Almost immediately, Spencer collapsed. Pandemonium set in as medics jumped into the ring to aid the stricken fighter. Within the space of half an hour, the earlier scenes of superficial glamour were violently replaced by the reality of the horrifying scene of a man lying prostrate on the canvas, battling for his life.

Within moments, the ring was packed with officials, security men, promoters and cornermen as a neurologist and doctor worked frantically to stabilise Spencer's condition.

Everyone, it seemed, wanted a piece of the action as, disgracefully to my mind, press photographers ignored impassioned appeals from both medics and security men to back off in order to give Spencer and those aiding him, the space they needed. I watched in dismay and disbelief as some of the photographers I had been working alongside during the contest moved in like hounds for the kill, refusing to give ground until they had taken further dramatic pictures, regardless of the cost to the welfare of the boxer concerned.

I had been attending the bill to cover Georgie

Smith's contest against Darren McInulty, Darren Bruce's contest against Harry Butler, and Hornchurch middleweight Jason Ratcliff's contest against Peter Mitchell.

Georgie, Darren and Jason have been featured frequently in my reports, and I have come to consider them as my friends. No doubt, had it been one of them laying there, these photographers would have acted in much the same way.

My mind flashed back to June last year, to a time when I was covering the progress of Havering-atte-Bower cruiserweight Dominic Negus as he challenged Chris Henry for his Southern Area title.

A cracking contest had ended with Dominic victorious but, like Spencer, Chris Henry collapsed in the ring and was rushed to hospital to have a blood clot removed from his brain. The awful scenes from that night were coming back to haunt the sport.

Although I did not know Chris Henry personally, I could not get him out of my mind until, weeks later, I heard he was making a reasonable recovery from his injury. Spencer, I know only vaguely, although I consider him to be a likeable young man. I have occasionally met him at the many bills I have covered over the years and, on occasions, I have interviewed him after his fights. What happened to Spencer touched me even more than what happened to Chris Henry, but only because our paths – albeit rarely – had crossed.

Watching ringside was Dominic Negus. He, if anyone at all, knew just what kind of emotions were going through Devakov's head at that moment in time. After what seemed ages, though it was probably only 15 minutes, Spencer was transferred to a stretcher and carried, unconscious, from the ring. Needless to say, the rest of the evening's boxing was cancelled.

Spencer was transferred to Charing Cross Hospital, before being moved to a London neurological hospital to have a blood clot removed from his brain. His condition, which was for the next three days described as 'critical, but stable' has, thankfully, improved. He has since regained consciousness and hopes are now high he will make a full recovery, although his boxing career is certainly over.

Last June, I found myself trying to justify this sport through the columns of this newspaper. That, at the time, was a difficult enough task in itself, bearing in mind what I had just witnessed.

Now I find myself in much the same position. I still maintain that boxers know the risks they may encounter. Everyone knows the sport can be dangerous. A ban, which has often been called for by the British Medical Association, would not solve anything. In fact, that would only force the sport underground – and the consequences hardly bear thinking about.

Boxing still has an awful lot to learn when

encountering a situation like it did on this particular evening. As Spencer was being treated, security men were seen to be arguing among themselves as to which way he should be taken from the ring – a situation that must be rectified urgently.

An emergency plan of action for times when things go wrong should be a priority for all promotions. It is not a situation to be dealt with as or when it arrives. Every second is vital if a stricken boxer is to be given the aid he requires.

I believe something must be done to ensure that only medics are allowed into the ring at such times. Everyone else is just another person in the way.

Some lessons do seem to have been learnt however. I remember reporting the scenes when Chris Henry collapsed at the end of his contest against Dominic Negus. At the time I criticised the apparent indecision and conflict between medics treating the stricken boxer in the ring. The treatment Spencer received while laying on the canvas seemed to be far better co-ordinated and a neurologist was present at the time.

Let's be honest, boxing can be a dangerous sport although, thank God, injuries such as those sustained by Chris and Spencer are rare.

The consequences of the events at the Royal Albert Hall are to be investigated by the boxing authorities. Let us hope then, that they will be

bold enough to implement any necessary measures
required to further safeguard the welfare of boxers,
no matter how unpalatable those measures may be
to those resisting change.

Nowadays, I see Spencer all the time. Thank God, he's
made a remarkable recovery. He looks so well. Even
now, although he'll never box again, when you see him
in the gym, working out on the pads, he looks just as
good as ever, and I know that when he looks at who is
currently fighting in what was his division, he knows
he could wipe any one of them out. Obviously, he's a
bit heavier than he was in his heyday but, believe me,
if you saw him in action in the gym, you'd think he
was phenomenal. He's so fit.

I admire Spencer so much. To come back so well
from what he went through is proof the man has such
a lot of bottle. Now he's at boxing shows as a pundit
for Sky television. He's a cheeky little sod – and such a
nice, nice guy.

As for the fight, Spencer's crew never under-
estimated his opponents. But Devakov didn't come
over here just to roll over. No, he'd arrived two weeks
prior to the contest, so he was really up for it. Often,
Russian fighters only arrive a couple of days before a
fight, but Devakov had prepared well and worked
hard against some really tough sparring partners – and
he'd really bashed them up too.

While the aftermath of the Chris Henry fight had
been a shambles, things had undoubtedly improved by

the time Spencer was injured – but there was still a lot to be done to improve safety measures for boxers.

Nowadays, I'd say ringside safety has improved dramatically. The British Boxing Board of Control has become far more involved and even the likes of people like me, working in the ringside security business, play an important role in this respect. Security at professional shows is a lot tighter these days. If a boxer is injured we ensure the ambulance personnel and doctors are the first ones allowed into the ring. If it's a big title fight, we only let a maximum of five people in each corner – or up to three in a non-title fight. Other than that, we won't allow anyone else in the ring and we always ensure there is easy access to the ring for the medics.

These days shows are not allowed to begin unless there are at least two ambulances present. Then, if one of the ambulances is required to transport an injured person to the hospital, there is always a spare vehicle in attendance. There had only been one ambulance when Chris was injured. That's why the decision to abandon the rest of the show was made on the night.

To be honest, I'd never really given a lot of thought to the dangers of brain injury in the course of my boxing career. I know Mum and Dad had concerns on my behalf, but I guess I was just fearless. I was more interested in making Dad proud of me and proving to myself that I could become a decent boxer. I just thought it was something that would never happen to me. Nowadays, however, as a family man, it would be more of a consideration.

Banning boxing would never work. As Ivan wrote, it would just go underground like it was years ago. I don't mean like the unlicensed circuit, far worse than that. I mean in dingey warehouses and such like. It's man's natural instinct to fight. Even my little girl will lash out if you try to take something she wants from her. It's a natural instinct. People aren't forced to box. It's a way of making a living – in some cases, a bloody good one. Others do it solely for the passion. It's a sport you either want to do or you don't.

Boxing, to be honest, has only brought me joy. I've had to face some hard times, of course, but it's brought me so much happiness. I just love to fight. And I've met some fantastic people through boxing. People like Chris Okoh – what a man. What a brilliant fighter he was. He's a probation officer now but, in his day, he was one of the best fighters I've ever sparred with. Scott Welch. Another good man. He's the most spiteful bastard you could ever meet in a ring, yet one of the nicest guys you could meet out of it. Promoters Barry Hearn, Frank Maloney and Frank Warren – all really good men.

Boxing's given so many bad boys a chance to make something of themselves. It's a man's sport. You don't get that many middle class guys or ex-public or private school boys taking up the sport. Those sort don't box because it's not in them. I am what I am. I'm a street boy with no airs and graces. A good boxer, but I learnt my fighting the hard way in the street. Being a tubby kid with glasses, I had to.

But ban boxing? Definitely not!

Chapter Eleven

ON THE ROAD TO A WORLD TITLE

Three months after the Chris Henry fight I was back in the ring, this time against Trevor Small at the Elephant & Castle Recreation Centre in Southwark. It was a real battle that ended as a draw, although I was convinced I'd won it. I wouldn't say I was holding back after what happened to Chris, but it was the only fight I never wanted to go to. I remember telling Lenny how scared I was that night and I don't even remember the first three rounds, at least not until Trevor caught me with a big right hook. From then on, I was wide awake and just went at him. I put him over in the last round and was sure I'd done enough to nick it, but I hadn't.

Next up was Konstantin Ochrej, a terrific Russian kid at York Hall. This contest was also screened live on Eurosport. I eventually stopped him in the sixth round, even though up till then he'd been clobbering the side of my face with such ferocity with right hooks I was really thinking I'd have to go down for the first time in my career because the pain was really killing me. At the start of the sixth, though, Lenny told me just to go out there and bash him up. So I did. With a solid left hook I broke his ribs. He sank to his knees and it was all over.

Bruce Scott at Picketts Lock, Enfield. That was one hell of a battle. He was coming in to the contest with 18 wins from his 20 contests – 12 of them knockouts. He was a real banger. By the end of the sixth round he'd really wound me up and we exchanged words, particularly after he hit me after the bell. I finished the eighth round with a cut under my left eye and he beat me in the ninth round on a stoppage. I'd lost my Southern Area title. But I've only got good things to say about Bruce. His body shots were the hardest I've ever taken. Even when he misses you the draught could put you down! That man is as tough as old boots. Once, when he connected, I thought he'd ripped my heart out.

Looking back, at the time I'd only had eight professional contests leading to this one, while Bruce already had around 20 under his belt – perhaps I should have taken things a bit more slowly before taking on a Southern Area title. This was a point made to me by Bob Longhurst of the British Boxing Board of Control. 'Once you win the Southern Area title,' he'd told me, 'there's no going back – you've no more time to learn.' He was right. From that point on, every fight would be a ten-rounder – all hard contests. Even my previous contest, against Ochrej, had been against a man who had smashed up Henry Wharton – though Wharton eventually got the better of him – and he'd also given Darren Corbett a good run for his money.

The place had been packed out for the contest against Bruce Scott but, despite all the support I'd had, I was feeling miserable. I felt I'd let all my supporters down. After I'd got showered and changed, I walked into the bar area. Lenny was already there and was looking just about as dejected as I felt. Then everyone started clapping and cheering. Some were even standing on their chairs. I thought Bruce had just walked in to join us. But, when I looked around, I realised they were all cheering for me and, even now, the memory of that moment brings tears to my eyes. Mum was there, so was The Tall Fella who came up to me and gave me a big hug. 'Dom,' he said, 'you were brilliant out there. You haven't let anyone down.'

In October 1998, I had several things going wrong in my private life, including splitting with a long-term girlfriend. I wasn't as focused as I should have been, plus I'd had to lose quite a bit of weight. As a result, I hadn't drunk enough water prior to my contest against Kevin Mitchell at the Broadway Theatre in Barking and, in the fifth round, my head was feeling pretty weird. I'd never experienced anything like it in the past and, thinking about what had happened to Chris

Henry, I became concerned the same was happening to me as the canvas seemed to be coming up towards me and everything seemed to be moving around. It was Frank who intervened to pull me out of the fight because he didn't like the look of me, not because I'm ugly, but because he could see I was in no state to carry on. He wanted me to go to the hospital afterwards but I refused. 'I'll be alright, don't worry about it.'

It was inevitable that my first professional defeat against Bruce would have dented my confidence to some degree, if only slightly, but it did affect my build-up to the contest against Kevin. I knew him pretty well as we'd often sparred together in the past and I'd often smashed him up, so I guess I was guilty of underestimating what he could do when it came to the crunch. I should have realised that all those rounds sparring in the Henry Cooper Gym in the Old Kent Road would also have given Kevin a good idea of my style, so he obviously put that to good use on the night.

The rematch four months later was for the now vacant Southern Area title and it was a complete and utter shut-out. Kevin never got a look in. I had him in the sixth round when he was really rocking. He sank to his knees, courtesy of a great body shot, but he made it to the end of the contest, which I won on points. I had reclaimed my title, but Kevin had certainly been up for it. He was so game. My performance had been boosted by my preparation for the contest. My sparring partner, Nicky Thurbin, had been a great help and it was his efforts that helped me out so much in training and that ensured I had the extra stamina required.

In May 1999, my preparations for a British title eliminator against the comically-named Chris P Bacon were ended prematurely in the gym at Five Star. It was that man Bruce Scott, a former British and Commonwealth champion who, not content with having beaten me just over a year previously, scuppered my hopes when he caught me awkwardly during sparring and popped one of my ribs. Told you he could pack a punch!

Next up was a British title eliminator against Chris Woollas at York Hall, Bethnal Green. I trained really hard for this fight, sparring with Montell Griffin. It paid off. I completely outboxed Woollas for ten rounds. So much for his trainer saying I was 'just a ruddy Southerner'!

Those last two fights had been by far the easiest of my professional career and made me appreciate Lenny more than I had. Bruce Scott, I realised, hadn't beaten me. *I* had. And it was all because I hadn't listened to Lenny. He'd been in my corner, telling me what to do, but I'd done my own thing and lost my title. Yet, by listening to Lenny and following his instructions to the letter when I fought Kevin Mitchell for the second time, and against Woollas, these seemingly hard contests turned out to be a lot easier than I had originally anticipated.

That said, I had a lot of problems professionally after winning the British title eliminator against

Woollas – so much so the title fight never materialised, and I even considered giving up the sport altogether. Bearing in mind how much I love fighting, this was not a choice I could have made lightly, but I was in fear of my life, health-wise.

I'd already witnessed what had happened to Chris Henry and Spencer Oliver – and now I was being plagued by dreadful headaches on a regular basis. With my style being more in your face, always prepared to take a couple of bangs in order to get in a few of my own, I knew the risks of sustaining a brain injury would be higher than for a more defensive boxer.

'This ain't right,' I remember telling Lenny. The sensible thing would have been to have followed his advice to get it checked out by a doctor straight away but, me being me, I kept putting it off and burying my head in the sand. Eventually though, it got so bad, I bit the bullet and made an appointment to see my GP. I wish I'd done so sooner because he soon diagnosed the problem – too much stress and caffeine.

Can you believe it – Dominic Negus being knocked out by too many cups of coffee! I'd been dehydrated. The signs had been there when I was pulled out of the first contest against Kevin Mitchell.

The delays caused by concerns over my health meant my chance to fight for the British title passed me by, much to my disappointment, and I was left to regret not having had my symptoms checked out much earlier than I did. Not only that, Bruce Scott was the

eased as punch in the minutes after being declared the winner of the Southern Area
le in 1999 after beating Kevin Mitchell on points.

Above: I like this picture. It was taken when I fought Chris Woollas at York Hall in Bethnal Green in September 1999 in a British title eliminator.

Middle: Woollas, left, and I slug it out

Below: My trainer Lenny Butcher offers a drink and some advice during my contest against Woollas.

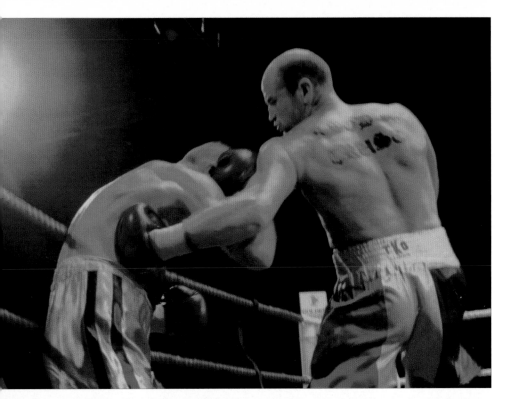

bove: Take that! A solid left into the ribs doubles up Garry Delaney when we
ntested the Southern Area title in October 2000.

elow: Garry gets one in on my head. A taste of my own medicine!

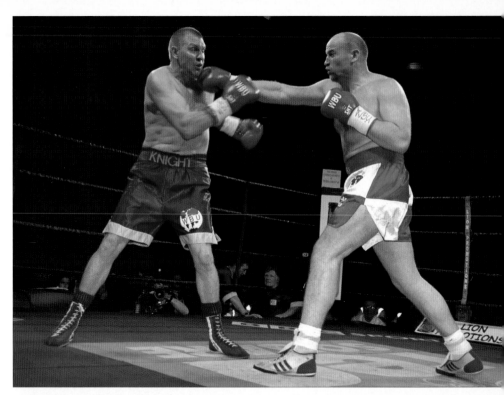

Above: Me versus Eddie Knight for the WBU Super Cruiserweight title in December 200[?]

Below: Proudly holding aloft my new acquisition! I now had my sights set on fighting a[s] a heavyweight.

and my pal Big John, below right, protested Vic Dark's innocence prior to my
test against Audley Harrison at Wembley in July 2002. My trainer Lenny Butcher is
tured below left. At the time, Vic was in HMP Hightown in Sutton after the police
nd a knife in the car in which he was a passenger. The TV company screening the
t insisted we remove the T-shirts, but, just as we were called to the ring, we put them
k on. Vic was really pleased his cause was supported on national television! Better
l, the police had nothing on him after all.

Above: I reckon I gave Audley Harrison a scare at the weigh-in by being so physically beefed up.

Below: Harrison hit me while I was down on one knee. That really riled me!

ove: I lost my temper with referee Ian John-Lewis and Harrison after that low blow.

low: Giving Harrison a good clubbing in return.

Above: The new IBA heavyweight champion! I've just beaten Jeff Temperley to win m[y] second world title. Left to right: Jeff Temperley's trainer, Jeff Temperley, me, my traine[r] Gary Bedford and Noel Tierny, and president of the Independent Boxing Association Alan Mortlock.

Below: Fruits of my labour. I'm pictured with the WBU cruiserweight world title belt, the IBA heavyweight world title belt, and the Roy Shaw belt. Today I'm out of the gam[e] I loved so much, and life hasn't stopped throwing challenges at me – but now I feel I'[m] fighting a winning battle.

reigning British champion at the time. That would have been a blinding rematch. If it had happened, I'd have fought him in just the same way as I had before, but this time, I would have listened to Lenny – and kept my hands up!

By the time I was ready to return to action, Frank Maloney had his hands full with two world champions, Scott Harrison and Lennox Lewis. These two were, unsurprisingly, his top priorities so I decided a change of manager could be a better option for me. Don't get me wrong – I can only speak well of Frank and everything he did for me. Everything he promised, he delivered. I just felt that a change at this time would benefit all concerned. I joined up with Dave Lewis's Golden Fists promotions company.

Dave's a top bloke who I would describe as one of my 'nicer' friends. He used to work for boxing promoter Frank Warren's Sports Network organisation where he'd worked his way up into a good position. Then he was offered the opportunity to work with a chap called Rodney Berman who was running a South African organisation called Golden Gloves which also had a British counterpart, Golden Fists, which used to promote Lennox Lewis.

Dave took up a position running Golden Fists. He already had some good fighters on his books, including Steve Bendall and WBU cruiserweight champion Sebastian Rothman. By signing up with Golden Fists, I knew my chances of challenging Rothman for his world title would be greatly enhanced.

Under Dave's management, a full year since my last contest against Woollas, I returned to the ring in August 2000 to box Tony Booth at the Whitchurch Leisure Centre in Bristol. I lost on points. Booth had been a very last minute replacement on the bill. In fact he was the third opponent lined up for me that night. I was looking at this contest as a warm-up for my Southern Area title defence. It proved to be a really scrappy affair and several of the spectators were booing Booth throughout because of his negative tactics.

At the end of the contest we awaited referee Dai Morgan's decision. To my astonishment he only awarded me one round out of the six. Even Booth was sympathetic afterwards and admitted that he thought I'd won it. Dave Lewis was incensed at what we considered to be the injustice of the decision. As for me, well, I drowned my sorrows at the bar with Booth and just had to be thankful it hadn't been a title contest.

Garry Delaney is another Essex boxer, a former Commonwealth title holder and, in October 2000, the holder of the Southern Area title. We both had strong followings so it was of considerable interest to the county's fight fans when we clashed at the Leisure Centre in Maidstone. Lenny and I had been planning ahead. After beating Delaney, I would have three or four more contests before, hopefully, getting into the frame to challenge South African WBU champion Sebastian Rothman for his world title. As it turns out, it doesn't always pay to think too far ahead in the boxing game.

I knew Garry was a good boxer, but he'd certainly done his homework on me prior to the fight. He knew I could easily lose my rag and set out to exploit it. Over the first three rounds I really thought I was going to stop him. Lenny, in my corner, was almost wetting himself, 'Come on Dom, you're gonna stop him.' But Garry kept winding me up and, true to his game plan, I was really getting the hump. 'Is that all you've got?' he'd say whenever I caught him good. So, I started dropping my hands and called to him, 'Come on then, fuckin' hit me!'

Bang, he did, and won the round, and the next, and the next. By now, I was losing the plot and bashed him hard in the bollocks – twice in fact – so I lost a couple more rounds, and he only beat me by a point. If I'd kept my cool, I could have beaten him, but that was down to me and my lack of discipline.

I take my hat off to Garry. He's a good fighter, and he turned out to be a really nice fella. He deserved to win on the night. It wasn't just the fight he won that night. Prior to being presented with the belt, Garry bent down on one knee in the ring and proposed to his girlfriend, glamour model Jodie Marsh, who accepted his proposal. I wouldn't say Garry and me are best mates, but I do consider him to be a friend. In fact, my hopes of challenging Rothman for his title came to nothing but, in March 2002, Garry took him on for the WBU title in South Africa. In searing heat, he was unfortunate to lose on a points decision. Garry's brother Mark is also a former boxer. A bloody good one too. A great guy.

My next fight was my first as a heavyweight, against Paul Fiske at York Hall in Bethnal Green. I beat him in the first round. Eamonn Glennon was next up. I won that one easily on points, 60-54. I changed tactics for this contest, using the jab and the uppercut much more instead of just going in for a tear-up. I really enjoyed the fight and Glennon only managed to hit me hard on a couple of occasions.

Eddie Knight stood between me and the WBU super cruiserweight title at the Goresbrook Leisure Centre in Dagenham in December 2001. With so much at stake, I'd trained hard for this one and came into the ring at 14 stone 10 pounds which was a terrific weight for me because I felt very powerful. Adam Wolf had been great during the build-up to the contest. We'd been sparring at Five Star every day and, as anyone would tell you, I certainly don't hold back in sparring! Eddie was a very good boxer and somewhat underrated. He'd been in with some good guys so I knew he was tough.

Like any other fight, there is no shortage of advice shouted out to the combatants from the crowd or from their cornermen. As a boxer, you can sometimes make out what people are calling out but, usually, I'm just focused, thinking along the lines of 'I'm gonna get ya.' However, a decent professional will always try to heed the advice of his cornermen.

Most times I was fighting I never missed the opportunity to glance towards my corner in order to receive any message or advice aimed in my direction, particularly as Lenny or Gary could often see something I could take advantage of or something I could be doing better. Sometimes it would just be, 'Keep doing what you're doing,' or, if it was beginning to turn into a bit of a battle, it could be, 'Okay Dom, just bash him up!' However, the advice I received during this contest was probably as good as I'd ever received.

The first round was really close and Eddie caught me with a couple of good, sharp shots, though not with any great power.

During the second round Dean Powell, who was working with Lenny in my corner, called out to tell me to hit Eddie with a left hook to the body. It was good advice – a left hook to the chin, followed up by another to the body, took him straight out.

At the age of 31, I'd become a WORLD champion.

Later that night we went to the Post House Hotel in Epping to celebrate. Everyone from Golden Fists was there, including my manager Dave Lewis and, of course, Lenny. My family joined in too, as did Sebastian Rothman who, earlier in the evening, had retained his WBU cruiserweight title after knocking out Crawford Ashley in the eighth round of their contest. Thankfully, Crawford was fit enough to come along too. All in all, I'd say we had a pretty good night.

I felt great but, surprisingly, it was a feeling that didn't last for long. I'd trained so hard for this fight and, suddenly, it was all over. It was the build-up that really did it for me, the anticipation and the prospect of having that belt put around my waist.

There were a few benefits of having a world title success behind me, although not as many as you may imagine. One perk, however, was a visit to Germany when Dave Lewis, a chap called Rodney Berman, and me were taken as guests to the Volkswagen Halle in Braunschweig to watch Dariusz Michalczewski beat Richard Hall in the tenth round for the WBO light heavyweight title. That was a good trip.

After feeling so great about winning a world title, it soon became a bit of an anti-climax. I'd been on such a high, but now I knew it could be weeks, or even months, until I got back into the ring. I reckon boxing's like my sex life – bang, bang, wallop and it's all over!

Thankfully though, I only had to wait a matter of a few weeks before I faced Paul Bonson in a contest at York Hall, Bethnal Green, reduced to just four rounds owing to time limitations on a double world championship bill. I won convincingly on a points decision.

Chapter Twelve

GET ME OUT OF HERE!

Some great boxers have come out of South Africa and, in 2001, Rodney Berman, of Golden Gloves, set it up for me to have a contest in Johannesburg. At the time of our departure Lenny and I had no idea who I'd be fighting when I got out there but we knew the fight would be quite a high profile one and, while there, I would be training in Nick Durandt's gym – and he was the number one trainer in South Africa. In fact, Nick had the biggest stable of professional boxers in South Africa. He'd trained more than 50 South African champions, including the legendary Sugar Boy Malinga.

We arrived in Johannesburg two weeks before the scheduled contest and were taken to our hotel from the airport. The hotel, although basic, was positioned within a lovely complex which was spoiled by the fact that its perimeter was surrounded with barbed wire – designed to keep out any 'unauthorised' visitors. Not only that, like many of the surrounding properties, the hotel had armed guards at the entrance.

Unfortunately, by the time we arrived, I had a bad stomach upset so there was no way I could have considered training that day. Although I never had a bite to eat all day, Lenny and I went to a restaurant that evening – after all, Lenny had to eat even if I couldn't. It was while we were in the restaurant that I witnessed something that sickened and disgusted me – racism.

A black waitress was serving a big fat Afrikaner who was talking to her like she was shit. I really didn't like it and told him not to talk to her that way. 'It's okay,' he replied, 'she's only a black, we treat 'em like slaves.' I told him what I thought of him, then realised the other Afrikaners there were just as bad as he had been. They all spoke very abruptly to the black people. That really gave me the hump and Lenny had to calm me down. From that point on, I knew this would be a real bummer of a trip.

Not only that, Lenny and I still hadn't heard from anyone at Golden Fists or their English counterparts Golden Gloves and, to tell the truth, I wasn't very happy about it. No-one had even bothered to check to see if we had arrived safely, and I'd really expected Joel Berman, Rodney's son who ran Golden Fists, to call me by this point. I still didn't know who I was supposed to be fighting or where I stood. Lenny decided to telephone a liaison officer from Golden Gloves to see what he could find out. We were told we were expected at Durandt's gym at 1pm the next day.

The following morning I intended to go running, but I was advised not to stray too far away because, such was the poverty in the area, there was a good chance I could be robbed for my trainers. Sod that, I thought, I'll run where I like, I can look after myself.

When I got back, a chap arrived in a beat-up old Volkswagen Golf to take us on the one and a half hour trip to the gym. En-route Lenny and I chatted to our driver. We'd heard there were some pretty rough areas in downtown Johannesburg and wondered where they were. 'Hang on, you'll see in a minute,' he said. Moments later we arrived at the gym in Bree Street. Welcome to the toughest part of town.

When we stepped out of the car we realised we were the only white faces around and it looked a really dodgy area. I told Lenny he'd better carry the bags, just in case I had to whack someone.

As we walked in to the noisy gym, it suddenly went quiet. The place had been buzzing as loads of black guys were working out, but now everyone had stopped what they were doing and were staring at us. All around there were posters and slogans. One read 'The harder you train, the luckier you get'. I spotted Nick Durandt who was working with a big heavyweight. Looking around, I began to feel uneasy, especially when I noticed some of the guys there were looking enviously at my Nike trainers. 'I don't like the look of this,' I said to Lenny. I'm not easily intimidated, but there were a lot of guys in there and they looked hungry.

Nevertheless, Lenny and I went on to have a good work-out on the pads and, before long, we got to realise that the lads there already knew who I was. In fact, they all made Lenny and me feel quite at home.

But it was while I was training there that I realised how cheap life in South Africa has become. We were aware of a commotion outside. Just a short distance from the gym stood a petrol station where three guys had turned up and tried to hold it up. Within moments, the police had arrived and shot them all dead. As we came out of the gym we saw three bodies covered over on the forecourt of the station. The value of life in Johannesburg, as far as we could see, didn't seem to mean anything.

We were taken back to our hotel on the outskirts of town. The complex was only a few hundred metres from the shopping area but we had been warned that, if we wanted to go shopping, the safest way would be to go by taxi or we could get killed by someone wanting our clothes. Having witnessed the poverty over there, it hardly surprised me that some people would take drastic measures just to get the sort of material items we take for granted. I was disgusted at the way the Afrikaners treated the blacks. Yet every black person we encountered was great to us. In fact, they treated us very well.

By the time I got back to my room I was feeling totally abandoned in this shithole of a place by Golden Fists. Fuck this for a lark, I thought. I want to get out of here. I decided to go to Lenny's room. I knocked on the door. Lenny opened it, standing there in his white Y-fronts. 'Are you alright Dom?'

'Do you like it here?' I asked him. He told me it didn't matter what he thought of the place. 'It's not the point,' he said, 'you're paying me to be here.'

'Well, I hate it.'

'Yeah, so do I.'

'Well then,' I said, 'I wanna go home.'

This really wasn't a place I wanted to be. I was so upset about the way the Afrikaners treated the blacks, and it just didn't *feel* right. It was just me and Lenny there, miles away from home. Maybe I'd have felt differently if there had been a crowd of us, but I doubt it.

I have to say, Lenny was a great support to me. 'Listen Dom,' he said. 'If you feel this bad, you're obviously not in the right frame of mind to box.' He telephoned Joel Berman back in England to tell him that I had the hump and that I wanted to come home but Joel reckoned I'd be passing up on a good opportunity of a high profile contest in South Africa: 'We could have sent someone else, but we decided to give Dominic the chance.' I took the telephone from Lenny so I could speak to Joel. 'Look,' I said, 'I hate it here, and I want to come home. Just book us a flight home.' I put the telephone down. Five minutes later, it rang. It was my manager Dave Lewis. Lenny answered it.

'What's up with Dominic?' said Dave.

'I don't think he's taken his pills,' joked Lenny trying to lighten the mood. However, after I'd spoken to Dave, he said, okay, he'd sort it out.

The next day at lunchtime we found ourselves at the airport, ready to come home. As we reached passport control, the guy checked my passport, looked up at me and saw I had only been in South Africa for three days. He asked why I was leaving so soon. 'Cos I fuckin' hate it here,' I replied as Lenny was frantically trying to shut me up and hurry me through before I could say anything else that might have got me into trouble.

When I got home the next day I received a telephone call from Joel who wanted to know when I'd be paying the bill. He reckoned it could total up to a couple of thousand pounds – but he still didn't bother asking how I was.

'Can you hear this?' I asked as I tapped the receiver loudly three times.

'What's that?'

'You've been knocked mate,' I said.

And that was the end of my relationship with Golden Fists.

Chapter Thirteen

CHEAT!

The WBU title win could have been my most notable moment in the sport but my boxing career really hit the headlines after what proved to be my most infamous bout – the final contest of my professional career in July 2002 at Wembley Conference Centre in which Olympic golden boy Audley Harrison was about to have a fight he'd never forget.

Let's make one thing clear: I don't like Audley Harrison. After winning the super heavyweight gold medal in the Olympics, everyone was falling over themselves to build him up. The BBC reportedly signed him up for a ten-fight deal, which, I think, was worth around a million quid, but he and his team took liberties, just taking on idiots and bums.

Because of that I'd always referred to him as 'Ordinary Audley'.

Then I was asked to fight him. I agreed, but a stomach bug sidelined me and my place was taken by Mark Krench. Eventually though, we got it on. Lenny arranged for a southpaw sparring partner as Harrison is also a southpaw. Trouble was though, I took the fight at such short notice and realised I was going to have real trouble reaching the weight. Harrison's camp must have been hoping I'd turn up at around 15 stone. In that case, he'd have a much better chance of taking me out. I decided I needed to build myself up quickly so began extra training with a bodybuilder.

Prior to the fight, I was really relaxed. To me, it was just another fight and I'm sure Harrison was nearly shitting himself at the weigh-in when I removed my top. All those lumps and bumps. Huge muscles. I weighed 16 stone 12 pounds – my normal boxing weight would have been around 15 stone. We had a proper head-to-head. I just wouldn't look away because I just don't like the fella. All I could think was 'left hook, left hook'. The cameramen said, 'Okay, that's enough boys,' but I still wouldn't take my eyes off him.

He turned away first. I've got your number, I thought.

I decided I'd dedicate this fight to a friend, Alison Kershaw, who had just undergone major surgery. I know you need guts to get into a boxing ring, but Alison's experiences had made me realise that she was ten times braver than me by the way she'd coped with everything. I was lucky to be fit and her situation had made me realise how precious life is.

I sold 600 tickets personally for this contest and, as I emerged from the dressing room at Wembley, I was greeted by a huge roar of support. Harrison, on the other hand, was greeted with more restraint.

When I hear all that cheering, just for me, I feel like the Incredible Hulk. I feel I'm massive, that I can't be hurt. Walking from the dressing room at Wembley I knew there was just no way Harrison was going to be able to hurt me. I just wouldn't allow it. It's truly an amazing buzz, which is why I can quite understand why so many boxers, the likes of Larry Holmes, George Foreman, and Sugar Ray Leonard, didn't want to retire because, once you are out of the limelight, you're history, and the limelight is like a drug. It's addictive.

And so to the fight. I still maintain that Harrison can't punch, even though he's a big lad. I have to admit though, at my heaviest, I was beginning to tire more than usual come the fourth round and I was getting pretty pissed off by Harrison leaning on me and regularly whacking me in the bollocks and the tops of my legs. That's when *IT* happened. Something that would grab the headlines and hit the TV news that night and the next day.

Harrison parried my right hook and my momentum sent me off balance and into the ropes. Harrison stepped back and the referee, Ian John Lewis, moved in. As I was about to get back up, Harrison moved in and, BANG, whacked me across the temple as hard as he could. If he'd really hurt me there's no way what happened next could have.

I was incensed and leapt to my feet. I spat out my gumshield and went face to face with Harrison. 'You black bastard, come on then!!!' Harrison laughed in my face and Ian stepped between us. Look, anyone who knows me would tell you I'm not a racist, no way. But in the heat of the moment, I guess that's just the way it came out.

But I wasn't finished.

'Laugh at me?' CRACK! 'Have that!' I'd nutted him and all hell broke loose.

Did I expect to be disqualified? You bet, and so did Ian who, by the way, I reckon is a brilliant referee. 'I'm gonna disqualify you,' he said.

'You try it and I'll fuckin' knock you out an'all!'

'Dom, Dom, calm down,' said Ian. I've got to give him his dues, in spite of all the furore at the time, he kept his nerve and took control of the situation. Then we boxed on. In the fifth round Harrison whacked me in the bollocks again. Ian stopped the fight to allow me time to recover. From that point on, the fight was a lot closer but, at the end of the day, Harrison got the points decision.

After the fight, which was watched ringside by my Dad, I decided I would, after all, go to Harrison's dressing room to congratulate him. I decided to take Dad, who was sitting in a wheelchair, with me. I knocked on the door which was answered by his security. I said we'd come to congratulate him, but the message was passed back that he didn't want to know. I told them I had my disabled father with me, but Harrison still wasn't interested. 'Tell him to go fuck himself then,' I said, as we came away.

I know it may sound like sour grapes, but I really haven't got any time for Harrison. I admit it was brilliant he won an Olympic gold medal. Good for him, but look how much more popular young Amir Khan is compared to Harrison. Khan returned from the Olympics with a silver medal before turning professional. But he's got two things Harrison hasn't. Flair and personality. Khan is exciting and modest. Harrison, although a good fighter, is cumbersome with attitude.

Fans love Khan, but how many really like Harrison? I'm sure there were several like me who were rather satisfied to see Danny Williams put him on his arse and beat him in December 2005. For too long Harrison had been believing his own press clippings and had consistently come across as The Big I Am but Danny brought him down to earth.

I'm sure Harrison hates me too because, although I lost the fight, I didn't lose the war. I exposed his limitations. For a start, he hasn't got a punch. That's not bravado on my part. You have to realise that when he hits you, there's 18 stones' weight behind it, but it just doesn't feel like it.

In our contest, at least for the first couple of rounds, he was sharp and showing some good footwork but, as for strength, sorry, but no. Prior to the contest I was sparring with light heavyweight Peter Oboh and, believe me, he hits an awful lot harder than Harrison.

I'm sure Harrison's camp didn't want me to have enough time to properly prepare for him, and they certainly got the hump when I pulled out of our first scheduled contest when I was ill, but there was nothing I could have done about that. Yet, even though I only had a few weeks' notice of our rearranged contest, I still sold far more tickets than he did.

I was sure I would be getting a kick up the arse from the British Boxing Board of Control for the headbutt, but nothing happened. A short while afterwards, in the real world, things were getting pretty heavy with the kidnapping episode, and this coincided with the time I 'escaped' to Tenerife. Back home, though, something had happened that would spell the end of my professional boxing career.

I first read about it in the national press. DOMINIC NEGUS FAILS DRUGS TEST. BANNED SUBSTANCE STANANOZOL FOUND IN URINE SAMPLE. I contacted my manager Dave Lewis. I told him it looked as if my piss test, taken on the day of the contest, had gone a bit wonky. He agreed, particularly as he'd just been talking to Robert Smith from the British Boxing Board of Control about me having a possible contest against Danny Williams.

Robert had told him, 'I don't think Dominic will be boxing any more for a while.'

During the time I'd spent in Tenerife, the board had been trying to contact me and were sending mail to my flat. I had to be punished. They gave me an indefinite ban and fined me £1,000. The story, I believe, first appeared in the *Daily Star* with a dirty great headline. My Mum saw it and was going mad, telling everyone it wasn't true, that her boy wouldn't do such a thing. On my return to Britain, I was denying I had deliberately taken any form of steroid, and described how it had been administered to me without my knowledge by the bodybuilder I'd been training with prior to the fight. I also let it be known that the bodybuilder had been made to pay painfully for effectively ruining my professional boxing career.

BULLSHIT!

By deciding to write this book I vowed to myself that I would wipe the slate clean. To make a fresh start. To be honest.

NOW FOR THE TRUTH.

I knew very well what I was taking in the build-up to the fight. I'd been desperately trying to pile on as much weight as I could, as quickly as possible and with the minimum decrease in stamina. Stananozol is an anabolic steroid and was one of several bits and bobs I was taking prior to the Harrison fight. I can't say I was too surprised to be caught out.

I can't plead ignorance any more. I knew what I was doing although, I have to say, when the test came up positive I really didn't expect it to be as obvious as it turned out. All the same, I was gutted and I knew this signalled the end of my professional career. My hopes of winning a British title at some point would now never come to fruition.

So there it is. I CHEATED. Even if I had beaten Harrison that night I wouldn't have deserved to.

Mum had spent so long denying I'd done anything wrong. I had to tell her, 'Mum, you'd better leave it. Don't worry about it, it's got nothing to do with you. Forget about it.' My relationship with Dad was more like best friends. I could tell him anything. In fact, it was immediately after the Harrison fight that I told him what I'd done. I told him that if, at a later date, he heard anything about it, he wasn't to worry himself. As usual, Bryn was totally up front with me when the news broke. 'You've just got to face up to it,' he said. Lenny gave me a proper bollocking and told me I should go to the BBBC, but I told him, 'Bollocks to 'em, tell 'em to fuck off!'

Looking back though, I wish I'd taken Lenny's advice. I still had so much more to offer professional boxing. If I'd paid the fine and served a ban, I'm sure I could have resumed my career as a professional by now. Looking at the cruiserweight scene at the time of writing, the facts are that I have a far more stable lifestyle and that the weight limit for cruiserweight has recently been increased to 14 stone 6 pounds, I'm convinced I'd have no trouble holding my own in the division. I'd even be confident fighting as a heavyweight at the moment when I look at who's out there. Apart from Danny Williams and Matt Skelton, there's no-one else out there.

But it's not to be. Having said that, I was told later by someone holding a relatively high-up position in the game's authorities that the only difference between me and many other professional boxers currently out there is the fact that I was the one caught out.

It's true I took the Stananozol with the bodybuilder I'd been training with. I also took two other substances, Winstrol and Sustenel, one being a growth hormone, the other to build up muscles. It also helps muscles repair more quickly. It provides a phenomenal recovery rate. Let's face it, I'd been around bodybuilding gyms long enough to know what would build me up in time for the Harrison contest.

Looking back, I really wish I hadn't taken the steroids. Had I gone in at my natural weight I would have been a lot faster. But, then again, I'd have been 15 stones, while Harrison would have been three stones heavier than me, and that's an awful lot to give away.

That's why I cheated.

On the other hand, I knew I could go the distance. I could keep going all day long (well, almost!) because I'm a distance fighter. Harrison isn't, but he's clever. He likes to lean on you, a tactic he uses to gradually wear you down as he transfers his weight onto you. The other thing he's got going for him is his massive reach advantage which makes it difficult to get in to him.

At the end of the day though, he won and he

deserved to. The fight only added to my notoriety – not necessarily because of the ban I received – but for the fact I'll probably be best remembered as the guy who headbutted Audley Harrison in the ring.

And I'm sure Harrison won't forget it in a hurry either.

There are a helluva lot of steroids out there in boxing generally. I know there are. Many top boxers use them. I've seen it first hand. Some top boxers who are lucky enough to have lucrative sponsorship deals can afford to use performance-enhancing substances because they also have the money to acquire the more expensive substances that can mask whatever they may have taken. These substances are known as blanketing agents. Of course, it's not just boxers who take such substances. I reckon men and women from a wide range of sports use blanketing agents but, I have to say, I think it's creeping more and more into boxing. The guys using performance-enhancing substances know that if they use blanketing agents prior to any drugs test they'll probably get away with it.

I reckon I had a pretty hard professional career. Just look at some of the guys I took on. Although I needed money to live on, it had never been my top priority. Mickey Duff once told me that, if I was coming into the sport just for the money, I'd be better off getting a proper job. Very true. I never made a fortune out of the sport. My top pay-out was around £7,500 for fighting Audley Harrison, and I only got £4,500 when I won the WBU world title.

Cheat!

But, for me, it was all about the fighting. Trying to prove to myself that I was no longer that fat kid from Woodford. I guess I learned to take my street smartness into the ring. Let's face it, I'm a street fighter through and through. That's where I really learned my trade, but I also learned the hard way in the ring. And I loved it. I was never happier than when I was either in the ring or in the gym.

On the streets it's just bang, bang, bang, but, when you're boxing, the chances are you'll be up against a guy who's just as fit as you are and who has a pretty good idea of what's going to be thrown at him. Like that, it's not often you can just slug it out with them. You *have* to use your jab – and some days you might even have to back off a little and be prepared to change tactics.

Of course there were the odd off days. As much as I enjoyed sparring with all the big boys, all the champions, there were occasions when I wondered if it was worth all the blood, sweat and tears.

Sparring is an integral aspect of professional boxing. While preparing for some of my professional contests I had the benefit of some pretty decent professionals who gave up their time to spend time in the ring with me. It works both ways. It gives both boxers the opportunity to keep fit and to try out their moves in a constructive way.

Often matchmakers like Dean Powell would telephone Lenny to enquire whether I was able to spar with one of their boys. Normally, it wouldn't be a

211

problem. Sometimes sparring partners get paid for their services but often, if they know the guy they're to spar with, they'll offer their services free of charge and will be happy just to be able to help out.

The list of my sparring partners is impressive. There were some terrific boxers amongst them. Mika Kihlstrom for instance. A heavyweight, he won gold in the Finnish championships as an amateur, and a silver medal in the European amateur championships before going on to become the WBB champion as a professional. He was a great sparring partner.

Mark Potter and I enjoyed some fantastic sparring sessions. Mark and I fought out of the same gym so we knew each other well. I reckon people would have paid good money just to watch us sparring. We'd always agree from the outset to take it easy but, before long, we always stepped it up and then we'd be slugging it out harder and harder. What a lovely fella Mark is. And he's quite a boxer. A former Southern Area champion, Mark lost to Danny Williams in a Commonwealth heavyweight title contest in 2000 at Wembley and, a year later, was beaten by Alex Vassilev for the WBU title. I really like him.

Then there was Peter Oboh. He's brilliant – and so underrated. Trouble is, no-one really likes to fight him because no-one's really worked out how he fights. A British-based Nigerian who was once ranked No. 2 in Britain and the No. 1 light heavyweight title contender, Peter won the British title in 2003 after he stopped Neil Simpson in the 11th round, and he won the WBA

International title a few months later when he stopped Elvis Michailenko in the 11th round. Peter's a bloody lunatic in the ring. Fight him and you feel like you're surrounded! Blimey, when we sparred together it took him two hours just to warm up!

Technically, Michael Sprott is probably one of the best fighters I've sparred with. I can't understand why Michael seems to lack confidence in his ability. He won the British and Commonwealth titles after defeating Danny Williams – and that's something I've never been able to do. He's also won the Southern Area title and the vacant EBU and WBF titles. I just feel he under-estimates himself but, as you can see, there's no reason why he should because he's a terrific boxer.

As for tough guys, Cathal O'Grady must be right up there. He's certainly one of the toughest boxers I've ever sparred with. We moved around together at the Henry Cooper Gym in Old Kent Road, south London. Cathal boxed for Ireland and won gold medals for his country. A southpaw, he was a big, big hitter – and was so awkward to spar with. I could really feel his power when I sparred with him and I had to give him full respect, even though as a professional, he didn't do as well as he might have hoped as he was knocked out a couple of times. That's the thing with some big hitters. Just because they can hit hard, it doesn't necessarily mean they can take a good punch back.

But Cathal was a hard man. If anyone's seen the pop video 'Rise Again' by Gabrielle they may well have spotted him. There's a boxing scene in it with a geezer getting bashed up – that's Cathal – and, in his corner, are boxing trainer Jimmy McDonnell and promoter Eugene Maloney.

In 1999, prior to his WBC light heavyweight title fight in Bremen, Germany, against Dariusz Michalczewski, from Poland, I sparred with American Montell Griffin. Griffin was a hard puncher with 30-plus knockouts on his record. He was a former IBF Inter Continental champion and a former WBU champion. He was also the first boxer to defeat Roy Jones Jnr.

But, on this occasion, Griffin had a huge task ahead of him. Michalczewski is a brilliant boxer. Just look at his record – more than 24 world titles in two divisions. Griffin and I sparred at the Lennox Lewis Gym in Hackney but our sessions ended when he and his team reckoned I was too mad because I just kept laughing at him when he was hitting me. For the record, Michalczewski stopped him in the fourth round.

I had some good sparring with Mark Delaney. As I mentioned earlier, Mark was a terrific boxer but he never really enjoyed the same success as his brother Garry. All I can say though is that had Mark had the same punch as his brother he'd have been a world champion – and he's got loads of bottle. Technically, I reckon he may have been even better than Garry.

Sparring with Scott Welch really opened my eyes as to what boxing was all about. I've already mentioned him, but he's worth a second go. What a spiteful bastard! He took no prisoners. He just wanted to knock you out. Sparring with him certainly made me remember to keep my hands up at all times, that's for sure! Outside the ring though, Scott's a great guy.

Alex Brawn. That man really gives me the hump! Guys like him are so lucky because whatever he does, he's bloody good at it. Alex is naturally gifted. He could do anything – play golf or practically any sport to a decent standard. He had a couple of amateur fights, and he's a top DJ. You could really hate a guy like that! But he's brilliant to spar with – just like a professional.

I'm proud of what I achieved as a professional. These days boxers can avoid those who pose the biggest threat but, when I started out, it wasn't like that at all. My professional career began with three second-round knockouts, then I was pitched twice in succession against the experienced Nigel Rafferty, who already had around 70 or 80 fights under his belt. A couple of fights later I was fighting for a Southern Area title. That just doesn't happen now. Guys are having 20 fights, getting, maybe, 15 knockouts against guys that can't even hold their hands up. I suppose that's possibly the best way to keep active and earning, but it was so different for me.

It's often said that professional sportsmen and women are role models to youngsters. Putting aside the time I cheated, I'd like to think that, boxing-wise, I was a reasonably good role model, particularly to the youngsters who trained at the gym but, unfortunately, some of them were aware of my life on the wrong side of the tracks – and some of them actually liked to hear about the more shadowy aspects of my life. That concerned me. If ever I heard any of them say they wanted to be just like me I always made a point of telling them that, as far as boxing is concerned, that's fine, but they would be better off concentrating on getting a decent education so they could qualify for a decent job – that they would need something to fall back on if they didn't make it as professional boxers. I didn't want them to try to emulate all my other failings just because they wanted to be like me.

My teenage nephew – also called Dominic – insists he wants to be like me. Dominic tells me that all his friends reckon I'm cool, so I've had to put him right. With just a couple more years to go at school, I've been trying to get it over to him that this is probably one of the most important times of his life.

I can understand why young people look up to top sports men and women. I did the same. My favourite boxer was Roberto Duran and, over the years, I've been lucky enough to meet a lot of top boxers although, I have to say, I've never been in awe of any of them.

When I began the security work, I found myself at London Arena in September 1990 when George Foreman came over to box Terry Anderson. Foreman knocked Anderson out in the first round. That night I met former British, Commonwealth, European and world featherweight champion Barry McGuigan. A terrific fighter. Barry was ringside in his capacity as a television commentator. I had always admired Barry but, as I was standing next to him, I realised we are all the same – two arms, two legs and a head.

No, I'm not in awe of any boxer – but I really admire anyone who has the guts to step into the ring. The same goes for women. If I'm honest, I can't say I particularly like to see two women fighting, but everything's changed these days and, as long as they're brave enough to do it and are trained properly, well, good luck to them.

I prefer grass roots boxers – the ones who climb to the top the hard way. Boxers like Steve Collins. Steve spent the early part of his career training in the same gym as Marvin Hagler in America. As a consequence, he wasn't widely known in Britain so, when he came to Millstreet to challenge the unbeaten Chris Eubank for his WBO super middleweight title in 1995, most people expected Eubank to beat him. After 12 gruelling rounds, Collins, known as the Celtic Warrior, won on a unanimous decision and went on to defend the title seven times.

Joe Calzaghe is another boxer I admire. I first watched him in Brentwood where he was defending his British super middleweight title against Mark Delaney. Joe is a really quick fighter while Mark had a much slower style. In the first round, Joe smashed Mark's nose up pretty badly, making it difficult for him to breathe. Nevertheless, Mark gamely battled on until the referee stopped the contest in the fifth round. Like Steve Collins, Joe wasn't widely known at the time but I knew that, as an amateur, Joe had won three ABAs at different weights and that he was a classy fighter so I'd had a bet on him to win.

Although I was in the money, I felt sorry for Mark – I love him to bits – but look at Joe Calzaghe MBE now – he's won British and Commonwealth titles, and the WBO title. He's come on leaps and bounds and anyone who witnessed the way he demolished Jeff Lacy over 12 rounds in March 2006 to unify the WBO/IBF super middleweight titles would bear testament to that. Joe was absolutely brilliant.

Chapter Fourteen

ON THE ROAD TO ANOTHER WORLD TITLE

With my own professional career now in tatters, there was only one way to go if I was to carry on boxing. I'd have to join the unlicensed circuit. After all, the BBBC were denying me the opportunity to earn a living. My main argument against paying their fine was, if I'm not boxing, I'm not earning, so how can I pay? At least the unlicensed circuit would help pay my bills.

Alan Mortlock is probably the top promoter of unlicensed boxing in Britain. I've known him for a good number of years now and we've become good friends. After my suspension by the BBBC he called me and suggested we had lunch together. During the course of our meeting I suggested he might like to promote me as an unlicensed fighter. He was pleased to take me on and, ever since, he's looked after me very well.

In many ways, the unlicensed scene is not so unlike the licensed scene. However, contrary to some rumours, unlicensed boxing is not illegal, although there are a few differences. Atmosphere-wise, I'd say it's probably a bit more exciting for the spectators and boxers alike. It's more intense. A bit rougher, perhaps. All boxers must have a medical check-up by a doctor before each fight and the St John Ambulance Brigade are in attendance. As in the pro-game, everyone's more on the ball these days as far as ring safety is concerned. There's no way an unlicensed promoter like Alan would allow a fight to proceed unless there were adequate medics, defibrillators and ambulances available in the case of any emergencies.

The most significant safety differences between the two codes is that, in the unlicensed scene, the boxers do not undergo an MRI brain scan before a fight and the match-ups between boxers are nothing like those in the professional circuit. There are often mis-matches. Sometimes, it's almost as if you can fight whoever turns up on the night! And there's plenty wanting to earn a few hundred quid for a night's work. Trouble is, half of them can't box sweets!

I know a guy who was about three stone heavier than his opponent who he put under a lot of pressure. Eventually, his opponent turned his back and it was all over, and the heavier guy was jumping around as if he'd won the world title.

On the other hand, there's some really good fighters on the unlicensed scene, many of whom use it as a stepping stone to get into the professional game. Trouble is, they can't box under their real names if that's the course they want to take because the BBBC won't accept boxers who have fought on unlicensed shows.

The BBBC still don't allow amateur boxers to spar with professional boxers either, nor do they approve of licensed and unlicensed boxers even sparring together – though it happens all the time. We're so out of touch in England. The Americans get so many good kids boxing in the Olympics because they have pro-am gyms. In England, well, we're light years behind them. Nine times out of ten, the Yanks have got the cream of the crop because that's the way they do things. I think England is probably one of the last countries where the boxing authority still won't sanction training between professionals and amateurs.

While I was fighting professionally, I often sparred with amateurs because it could be tricky finding fellow professionals who were available. So what are you supposed to do? At the end of the day, if an amateur sparred with me, it benefited both of us – I had some useful training, and he got to learn a few tips of the trade from me. What's so wrong with that?

I finally burned my bridges with the BBBC when I turned out as an unlicensed boxer, but I found it easy pickings. My first opponent, Roger Toon, was a European kickboxing champion. Credit to him, we went the distance and I won on points.

When I first turned professional, everybody would come along to cheer me on – businessmen, councillors, loads of friends but, because I was now boxing on the unlicensed circuit, some of the bigwigs didn't come along any more because the scene had a kind of black mist surrounding it and I guess there are a lot of people out there who still think unlicensed means illegal. Nevertheless, in spite of all that, I've enjoyed some great support against Toon from faithful fans who have watched every one of my fights throughout my career.

After the fight I had the opportunity to spend a few weeks in Spain. Nick Cole and his mother had a little flat on the outskirts of Alicante which was offered for my use. All told, I was out there with Nick for six weeks. But that didn't mean I let my training slip. Nick is a good pad man so we spent quite a bit of time training in the nearby Europa gym.

I really loved it out there and I got to meet some really nice people, workers mostly, and the pace of life was so much more relaxing.

One day, while Nick and I were training, we became aware of someone standing by the doorway watching us. I wondered who he was. 'Hello mate, you alright?'

'Yeah, fine.'

It was obvious from his accent that he originated from the Birmingham area. Nick and I continued working the pads. Then the guy said, 'Can I ask you a question – are you Dominic Negus?'

'Yeah, I am.'

'Fuck me, I've just been reading about you in a book!'

He joined us and, once we'd got to know him, we gave him the nickname The Northern Connection. Together we all went for a drink in a nearby Irish bar called Paddy's. When we arrived I noticed a chap called Jean Paul, a familiar face to regulars to the bar. Jean Paul was a bit of a flash git, but very clever – he could speak several languages.

Nick, being Nick, soon spotted a load of teenage girls, American, I think, and he fancied his chances. I should say that Nick is ten years younger than me, so the girls were of little interest to me but, as Nick is such a smashing lad, I slipped him some cash so he could offer to buy the girls a drink and, before long, he was having a great time. Meanwhile, I was sitting with a guy called Bastian who owned the bar, and a woman called Lola who, for the past few nights, had been trying to help teach me to speak Spanish. We had a good evening and decided to return the following night.

Again, Jean Paul was in the bar. Then Nick arrived with an American girl on his arm. Seems his charms the previous evening had borne fruit. I bought some drinks. Then Nick, who had already had a few elsewhere, wandered up to Jean Paul, put his arm around his shoulders and said, 'Hello Jean Paul, are you alright mate?' and offered to buy him a drink.

What Nick didn't know was that earlier in the evening, Jean Paul had already had a few too many and had been involved in a heated row with some

American customers. Furthermore, he didn't take too kindly to Nick's friendly offer. 'Do I know you?' he demanded.

'Course you do, I'm Nick.'

'I don't know you, take your arm off me. It's lucky I like you else I'd give you a slap!'

I intervened and told Jean Paul to be nice to Nick because he was a good lad and he had only been trying to be friendly, but Jean Paul's response was to offer me a slapping as well. I told him that if that was what he wanted to do he should get up off his arse and try it. He got up and wandered over to me: 'What are you gonna do then?' he asked me.

Now bearing in mind I'd had plenty of troubles back home and had been looking forward to getting away for a few weeks' peace and quiet, this was a situation I hardly needed but, on the other hand, with Jean Paul walking right up to me, there was no way I was prepared to give him a free shot, so I nutted him – CRACK! – and he fell spark out onto the floor.

Within seconds, I'd been surrounded by angry bar staff and customers. It seems Jean Paul was their blue-eyed boy. 'But you saw what happened,' I protested. A friend of mine, Mike, spoke up for me. 'The guy was out of order,' he said. 'You don't challenge people like that and expect to get away with it.' But it was obvious I'd upset a lot of people. I went downstairs, practically in tears. I'd been trying so hard to stay out of trouble but, as far as the people in the bar had been concerned, it had been *my* fault. It was *always* my fault.

Nick walked home with me. 'I'm so sorry Nick,' I said.

'No, thanks Dom,' he said. 'I thought he was gonna beat me up.'

I had a bad night's sleep. The next day I was wondering what we could do, because although we'd been to that bar most days I didn't fancy going back so soon, but Nick was having none of it. 'You haven't done anything wrong, Dom. Let's go back.'

As we entered the bar we got the evil eye from just about everyone and hardly anyone was prepared to speak English. I was distraught. What had I done?

I spoke to Bastian. 'I'm really sorry, I don't know what to do. Is he okay?' Bastian telephoned Jean Paul and passed me the receiver.

'Hi, Jean Paul, are you alright mate?'

'Yeah, but I don't know what happened.'

I asked him to come to the bar so I could apologise properly and buy him a drink but he refused, saying he was too scared to face me again. Eventually, though, I persuaded him that he had nothing to worry about.

When he arrived he was sporting a huge lump above his eye and his face was badly bruised. We sat down. 'What happened?' he asked.

'Don't you remember? You said you were going to give me a slap and you were slagging Nick off?'

'What? – why would I want to do that? Nick's a lovely boy. I can't remember a bloody thing!'

I returned to England in time to prepare for my second unlicensed contest, this time against Paul

Somerfield. I knocked him out in the third round. I was back earning money in the ring but, without the support of a sponsor, Lee Chisholm, who owned a glazing company, I wouldn't have made much of a living out of it. Lee gave me money for each contest, while Ray Coleman, who ran one of the biggest breakdown recovery businesses in Britain, Lantern Recovery Specialists Plc, stumped up cash for each show. Micky Theo, who ran the KO Gymnasium, was also a great help. He allowed me full access to his gym, free of charge. In fact, I reckon Micky could have been a really good fighter himself. He was often sparring, although we never sparred together. If we had, it would probably have been a real tear-up because I don't hold back, and neither does he!

Having fought professionally for so long, I couldn't help thinking the guys on the unlicensed circuit were not in my class. Until, that is, I let my standards slip. At the time my Dad was seriously ill in hospital and it was in the wake of the armed kidnapping arrest. Just like the time when I first fought Kevin Mitchell, my heart wasn't in it when I took on Karl Barwise at the Circus Tavern in Purfleet. I was out of shape, out of sorts – and beaten on points. Worst of all, the fight had been featured on a television documentary.

The next day I visited Dad in hospital. He was concerned because I'd lost the fight. I told him not to worry. That it had just been a bad day at the office.

The following day, Dad died.

It was a few weeks earlier that a friend of a friend

came up to me and mentioned that a television company wanted to film a documentary for the BBC about someone who was living their life on the edge of the law. Would I be interested? 'Okay,' I said. The producer, Nick Godwin, and a film crew came to see me. I told them that, since the kidnapping aggro I'd been thinking about cleaning up my act and, looking back, I don't really know why I agreed to go along with it, but I did. I guess I just wanted to set the record straight. The filming lasted around three months. They were mad. They wanted to come on some debt collections with me, but I wouldn't let them. At the time, Dad was lying in a hospital bed, dying of cancer. Trouble was, some geezer and his missus had fleeced Dad out of thousands of pounds. This was personal and, probably against all common sense, I set up a meeting with the guy at Dad's place near Clacton-on-Sea and allowed the film crew to come along.

Knowing I wasn't too happy with him, I have to admit the guy had some bottle to actually turn up. At first he didn't know there'd be a film crew there so I reckon he probably felt a bit safer knowing everything was being filmed. A big mistake.

The guy was scum. He owed money to lots of people, but he owed my old man around £10,000 and now he was trying to get away with it. Even though the cameras were rolling, I wasn't having that and got a little heavy with him. I gave him a bit of a slap and put his head through Dad's bathroom door. So what? He wasn't exactly going to press charges against me was he? The geezer was a dog, and his missus wasn't much better.

While Dad was in hospital, Mum, who was now separated from my Dad, was helping to sort out his finances for him. Going through the statements she discovered the woman had been squeezing money out of Dad on a regular basis, 200 quid here, 300 quid there, adding to almost £30,000 altogether. From what Dad had been able to tell me, the geezer had come round to the house and begged him for money and even rang him with threats. That's why I took this one so personally. Dad, meanwhile, was worried I'd get into trouble while trying to recover the money. Demanding money with menaces carries a hefty sentence.

Well, did I get the money back? I had to decide how far I was going to take it. Would I have to *really* hurt him? Or should I let him spend the next few years looking over his shoulder? And what about his wife? She'd given Dad grief as well.

Trouble is, they've got two kids and, since I'd become a father, my outlook on life had changed considerably. I didn't fancy marking him because his kids would have to look at his face for the rest of his life and I didn't want them to look at him and see me. With the cameras there, I had to tread more carefully. I told him I'd be back.

'I'll pay, I'll pay,' he assured me but, while I was in Tenerife recovering from the gym attack, they did a runner. They've since completely disappeared. It'll keep though. I'll bump into him again some day.

During the documentary I was asked if I'd ever killed someone. I smiled at the camera, paused for a long, long time, then said no. It was a deliberate ploy to keep 'em guessing. To promote an aura of sinisterness. Is that a word?

Of course I haven't killed anyone, although I've come close to it on occasions. My cagey response to the question was just what they wanted to hear. If I'd said there and then that I'd never done anything wrong it would have been the end of the interview.

It was funny to see the finished documentary, the way it had been edited. Some of the first interviews appeared in the middle or at the end of the programme and vice-versa. It's just how they wanted it to come out I guess. It's like some of the so-called hard man books where guys are boasting about the people they've killed or shot. In some cases, it's only in there to enhance their tough guy status. It's not necessarily true. It's just for the image and to sell books.

In writing this book, for instance, there are things I couldn't possibly put into print about what I've done. That's the difference. There are things about me I'll take to my grave. I won't be bigging them up just to make me look that bit harder than other villains or to sell more books.

The documentary included my defeat against Karl Barwise and the aftermath of the gym attack. There were shots of the blood all over the dressing room floor and then they filmed me as I walked out of the hospital the next day looking like Tutankhamun. I guess they couldn't have wished for better footage than that. The documentary ended with me saying how I wanted to clean up my act. How I wanted to walk away from my violent lifestyle.

Its screening had a huge impact on people who know me. Several of them have commented on how surprised they were that I'd allowed my actions to be filmed in such a way. Some wondered how my Mum would react to seeing me acting so violently. Well, all I can say is, to Mum, I'll always be her little soldier.

Joe, one of the guys who trains in the gym, saw the documentary on TV. So did his girlfriend who couldn't understand why Joe would ever want to hang around with me. 'He's an animal,' she said. Joe admitted that, when he first met me, he thought I was just a bully but, now he knows me better, he reckons I'm just the opposite.

I suppose the documentary was quite an accurate portrayal of me as I was at the time, although they only showed what they wanted the viewers to see. I wasn't too unhappy with the final cut, although I was more unhappy with myself, the way I came across on screen. Believe it or not, I have made a conscious effort not to swear so much since the screening which was full of f-this and f-that. I'd hate it if my little one was to grow up speaking like that. Take Lauren – she's the sweetest girl you could meet, a bit cheeky sometimes, but she's brilliant. As for Annabella, well, with parents with personalities like me and Nic, there's probably trouble coming in future years!

There's another documentary about me which was filmed in 2005. This one was part of a series called *Britain Behaving Badly,* which is shown regularly on the Men & Motors television channel. This one came about after boxing reporter and presenter Steve Bunce phoned me to let me know there was a television documentary producer looking to interview a 'hard man' and would I be interested in giving her a call?

Her name was Isobelle, a nice lady. She reckoned I fitted the bill perfectly and assured me the programme would show me in a reasonable light. On film I was interviewed about the debt collection work I'd done in the past and described how, in a space of just one week, I'd knocked out 18 people. Now that ain't normal is it? How could they possibly have shown me in a good light after coming out with that?

Following the gym attack I had to turn things around boxing-wise. The first couple of fights were a bit heavy-going but then I began taking things more seriously, running again. Gary Bedford resumed training me. Next up was Ginger Hooper, a kickboxing champion. A left hook downstairs after just 35 seconds ended his challenge.

My next opponent was one of the strangest I'd ever faced in the ring. Harry van der Meer is the No. 1 bodyguard in Holland and it's easy to see why. He lumbers in at 28 stone. He's 6' 5" high and is a cage fighter. He took me the distance, but I won on points. I have to say though, Harry's one of the nicest blokes you could meet – and the toughest son of a bitch to boot.

231

Then it was a Russian geezer – a world contact karate champion whose name I can't remember. He went over after just 40 seconds in the first round. Then I lost a bit more weight and boxed another Russian, Nicholai, who had boxed in the Olympics. He was one of the best guys I'd been pitched against but I put him down in the first round, then smashed him up for the next five and won on points. John Sheridan was my next opponent, but it didn't last long. I put him down in the first round and finished the job off in the second.

My performances earned me a shot at the IBA world heavyweight title. Jeff Temperley stood between me and the belt, but not for long. I finished him off in the fifth round. The hard training and work with Gary had paid off.

I love boxing but, on the unlicensed circuit, I was becoming frustrated at the standard of opponents put before me. I began to think about calling it a day. But then, in December 2005, I got the opportunity to put the record straight against Barwise, this time fighting for the Roy Shaw belt. Just before the bell for the first round Gary said, 'Dom, this one's for your Dad.' Barwise didn't know what hit him that night. I finished him off in two rounds, doing a better job on him than Joe Calzaghe managed. After receiving the belt, I took the microphone and announced my retirement from boxing.

My performance that night caused several spectators to question the wisdom of that decision. I was told it had been the best performance some had ever seen from me. That I looked a million dollars. How could I possibly consider packing it in after a display like that?

But I've got out at the top. Don't get me wrong, I love boxing, but I'd just won two belts in successive months, the world title and the Roy Shaw title. Roy was in the ring with me when I was presented with the belt. I told the spectators that I'd just won a title that meant more to me than the world title I won on the professional circuit. Roy couldn't believe it and I think he was quite emotional at the time. But it's true. He's someone I've always aspired to. Him and four-times Irish amateur champion Joe Egan. They were both fighters who wouldn't take backward steps.

I've known Roy since I started working the doors. He's a good man with good morals, real old school. It's not like that any more.

It's the same with Joe. In some ways he reminds me so much of myself. I've known him for some years through the boxing trade and he really was one of the very best Irish fighters. He's had a lot of grief in his life, but he's stuck to his guns and never walked away from anything – although he was never a troublemaker. Unfortunately, there are not a lot of people around like Big Joe Egan.

My earlier defeat by Barwise had been eating away at me because I know I'm a fucking good fighter and, if I'd not been so out of shape when we first got it on, if I'd have done things the right way, I'd have beaten him for sure.

But now I was the No. 1 on the circuit. No disrespect

to British champion Johnny Smith but Johnny who? He's not going to be any better than anyone else I've fought before. There's just no one out there for me now. I've been in with Audley Harrison, I've sparred with Montell Griffin and all the big Russians, Julius Francis and Scott Welch, so the prospect of fighting Johnny Smith doesn't particularly excite me, although I've given my promoter Alan Mortlock the nod to keep the door open for me to go to Wales to fight Smith if he wants to take me on in a year or so but I'm not just going to hang around on the circuit waiting for him. I just can't be bothered with all that. Nowadays, when I go to the gym, I just want to move around in the ring. I want to fight. I'm not too bothered about running and skipping any more.

I know I could have carried on for several more years had I wanted to. The way I was performing over those last eight months, no one could touch me. All my last few fights had ended as knockouts – two in the second round and one in the fifth – easy fights because I'd trained hard enough to make them so. I wish I had trained as hard for Lenny as I did for Gary Bedford. I was sparring with class fighters like Matt Skelton and Phil Soundy – and I was handling them pretty well.

Even though I'd been fighting really well at the point of my retirement, I still don't think I ever really reached my peak. While training with Gary I was fighting regularly – every eight weeks normally. That's five fights in ten months. The longest break I had was three months, and that was only because there were no shows. It felt so good. Phenomenal. I was on fire. Gary reckoned I brought such a reputation to the ring: 'Even if you do have a bad day, you'll probably still win with a knockout.'

At the end of my career I'd never enjoyed my training so much and I was far more focussed because of what I had to lose. When I was a single man without any commitments, it didn't matter too much if I lost a fight. I could just clear off somewhere for a week or so to recuperate, feel sorry for myself or lick my wounds.

Not now though. Now I have a baby, partner and stepdaughter to support.

But that doesn't mean to say I don't miss the involvement in the game at all. Sometimes, when I'm working at a show, I get the pangs to climb back into the ring but, I have to say, I don't miss the pressure I used to put on myself before and during each fight. Let's face it, as a former professional boxer and world champion, a lot was expected of me every time I fought on the unlicensed circuit. Fair enough, I suppose, but I was in a no-win situation because of it. If I won, well, in most people's eyes, I should have. But, when I lost first time round to Barwise, that didn't reflect well on me at all.

And that's why it was so important to me to do the job properly the second time we met.

Chapter Fifteen
IN GOD WE TRUST

Mum and Dad split up when he was 76. Dad reckoned Mum was going through a mid-life crisis. At the time, I was living in Lenny's flat in Havering-atte-Bower on the outskirts of Romford. Mum moved into a bedsit and, in 1996, Dad bought a mobile home in Jaywick, near Clacton-on-Sea. Then Mum moved again when she bought a place in Loughton.

They never divorced though because Dad told her that, if they did, she wouldn't get all the benefits he'd worked all his life for. It was a very amicable split. Even a few years later, when Dad was dying in the hospital, Mum would come and visit him. Mum's boyfriend Chris – a nice fella – used to come along too. Dad was always worrying about Mum, wondering how she was getting along, if she was alright. I reckon it's just that the age gap between them was too big.

Of course I'm close to my Mum. No one will ever hurt her as long as I'm around. As for Dad, to be honest, I can't really say I ever started chatting meaningfully to him until I was 26 when I turned professional. Before then I was usually in my room listening to music, basically just doing my own stuff. That all changed when Mum and Dad split up. I really felt for Dad living on his own in Jaywick. I became a lot closer to him and, I think because I was boxing, he seemed quite proud of me as I was doing something he'd always wanted to do. I've been very lucky to have met so many of my heroes, but none of them were anything compared to my Dad. I guess I was in awe of him.

I sometimes think it's little wonder I turned out the way I did. After all, I always aspired to be like men who lived on the fringe. People like street fighters Roy Shaw and Lenny McLean and Irish amateur world champion Joe Egan.

Then there's Vic Dark. This geezer's a legend. And very popular with Her Majesty too it seems as, for several years, it's been her pleasure to accommodate him behind bars. Prison bars, that is.

I was fortunate to meet Vic through a mutual friend and, if you didn't know anything about his past, you'd be thinking he was a proper gentleman. Vic used to train at the same gym as me, although at the time I didn't have a clue who he was. The first thing I noticed about him were the tattoos on his legs. Then, one day, my mate came in and asked me if I'd seen Vic.

'Who?'

'The geezer with the tattoos.'

'Yeah, he's upstairs.'

After a while, Vic came back downstairs and sat with us. From that day on we just clicked. Even though he's spent so long in prison, he's as fit as a fiddle. He's a martial arts expert, and he can have an almighty tear-up if needs be. He'll do anything for you.

He's another person whose loyalties are undivided. He's one of those blokes who, if ever you did any work with him, you wouldn't have to check your share of the cash because he'd give it to you fair. That may surprise some people, particularly bearing in mind his criminal background.

Yes, Vic's been in plenty of trouble in the past. He's served 19 years for armed robbery, and was an enforcer for some of London's most infamous gangsters. At Parkhurst Prison he was considered to be one of the hardest inmates.

In the past, Vic was partial to robbing banks. That's the only thing that makes him different from most blokes who go out to work. Robbing banks and post offices was his job. He wasn't bad at it apparently. It's just that he kept getting caught.

Then there was the time when a robbery went tits up and ended with Vic taking an Irishman, a Chinese chef and a copper as hostage in a police car. They done him for that too.

Even though Vic and I don't see each other so often, I consider him to be one of my closest friends, a point I was keen to make clear when he was arrested after police stopped a car he was travelling in and found a knife in its glovebox. They reckoned he must have been on his way to a job and he was put on remand. Prior to my contest against Audley Harrison, I wore a T-shirt with *Vic Dark Is An Innocent Man* printed on the front. How true. In the end, the Old Bill had nothing on him and had to drop the charges against him.

Now Vic's a reformed character and, amongst other things, he writes books. Two of them, *How To Rob Banks and Influence People* and *Into the Heart of Darkness* have been produced by Blake Publishing and are well worth a read – that should keep my publisher sweet!

Vic has proved he can live his life in a better way. If he can do it, why shouldn't I? These days, when I wake up, I look at Nic and feel I should pinch myself. I thank God for the day I met her. Nic used to work in a coffee shop in Queens Road, Buckhurst Hill. That's how I got to know her. I often used to pop in for a coffee and a bit of breakfast and, after catching sight of Nic, I suddenly became a much more regular customer.

We began going out together just before I was due to fight Paul Somerfield in my second unlicensed contest. Trouble was, I had previously booked up a six week break in Spain for immediately after the contest and I wasn't sure how Nic would feel about it if I were to disappear for so long so early into our relationship.

We agreed to telephone each other each day, which we did, and I guess I fell in love with her over the telephone which is really weird, especially as sometimes we'd rowed! If ever that happened, I'd just say, 'Nic, I'm gonna start afresh,' and I'd put the phone down. Then I'd ring her straight back and say: 'This is Dominic, I'm very pleased to speak to you!'

By the end of that six weeks in Spain I could hardly wait to get back to see her. I love that girl so much – I just couldn't be without her. To be honest though, if Nic had known more about me before we met, she wouldn't have touched me with a bargepole. She's told me that. When we first met she had no idea who or what I was. It was only later on in our relationship that she began to hear things about me but, by then, I wasn't really like that any more. The way Nic sees it, I'd never hurt her or the girls. She's made me realise what a lie I'd been living for so long.

After all, what's a bad reputation worth? I remember philosophising over this very subject with The Tall Fella. He's a skinny bloke with a skinhead and a very dry sense of humour. If you didn't know him well, you'd be unsure how to handle him because, if he doesn't like the look of you, he'd be pan-faced and wouldn't really talk to you. But, break the ice, and he's a nice fella.

For a while I spent around six months kipping on his mum's sofa. The Tall Fella and me used to do just about everything together. We went away together, worked together, and fought together. We had a particularly tricky situation together once but, somehow, we're still here to tell the tale! We don't see as much of each other these days but not for any particular reason. People just tend to go their own ways sometimes.

Normally, The Tall Fella's got really good morals but there was a time when we were both as lost as each other. I remember we were talking about the reputations we'd been trying to establish for ourselves. This was around the time we'd both be recognised almost wherever we went. Club doormen would let us in for nothing, and people would buy us both drinks.

'We're there now, aren't we?' I remember him saying.

'Yeah, but I didn't realise it would as tough as this,' I replied.

I'd just begun to realise that respect and fear are two completely different things – and a lot of it was down to fear as far as people's attitudes to us were concerned.

We'd just become horrible people. Of the two of us, The Tall Fella was the one who would usually do all the talking when we worked together collecting debts. Me? I just did what I did. All the same, The Tall Fella and me have had some good laughs in the past but, when I cut my wrists, well, he just couldn't handle that at all.

When I was single I didn't give a fuck about anyone or anything. If I got arrested, so what? But then Nic came along and I had to do something. I didn't want to put myself into any situation that could conceivably result in us being forced to spend time apart. Nic made me realise what I'd been missing all along, how much I had to lose. I've had previous relationships, but they were nothing to what I've got with Nic. Now, I don't feel as if I'm on my own. I feel safe now.

There were times when I needed to compete against people who I felt had flash homes or cars, particularly if someone inadvertently had rubbed my nose in it. There were often occasions when such a situation would cause me to do something silly.

While working in Birmingham at the UB40 concerts, Big Dave and me decided that, rather than staying in hotels, we'd stay at Kev and Paul's homes. I stayed with Kev, Big Dave went to Paul's. It was while I was at Kev's that I fully got to appreciate what a great family man he is. He's got two sons and a daughter, and a lovely wife. Watching them all together reminded me of Lenny McLean who always insisted that, for all his violent deeds, his kids loved him just because he was 'Dad'.

It was the same with Kev. His kids were all over him, kissing him and he was obviously enjoying playing with them. Brilliant. Outside his front door, for all his kids knew, Kev could be a horrible bastard when the going got tough but at home, just like Big Dave, they're just 'Dad'.

I've realised that's how I should be with my family. I've realised it doesn't hurt to say sorry to someone. It doesn't hurt you to laugh with people or even if they laugh at you. At one time, that would have really given me the hump, but not now. I'm thicker skinned. Trouble is, it's taken me 36 years to realise it! Sometimes Nic asks me why I say sorry so often. I tell her I don't know, but I've got 36 years to make up for!

It's funny how life can go full circle. One minute you're a baby, then a boy, then a man. You get involved in this or that, then you walk away. I often go in to look at my baby sleeping and I think how lucky am I? I guess Him upstairs put me through all the aggro to make me realise what real life is all about.

Nic is my life. She has made me the man I always knew I could be. She has made me realise that it's okay to laugh and also to cry. She is someone who loves me for me, not what I can do for her and, when she smiles, I just melt! She gave me Annabella and, that alone, is so, so great. Just to see that little girl grow before my eyes is such a miracle. And, of course, Nic brought Lauren into my life too, and what a great girl she is. With these girls on my side, I know I can't go far wrong.

I'd thought things for me would have been so different to what they are now. My fantasy had been to own a little house on the coast, somewhere like Devon or even in Spain. I thought I could walk along the beach, just me, Nic, the kids and a couple of dogs on a cloudy, drizzly day – who needs the sun? – with the waves crashing around us. I thought I'd be the world champion with a bank account full of cash, a nice house and flash car, the lot. But, even though I

244

haven't got the riches I'd predicted, I still feel I'm like a millionaire.

I may be poor in pocket but I've got everything a man could need when it comes to family. I realise now they're the same people who were around me during my troubles. Thing is though, I was so fucked up, so blind to all these wonderful people when I was getting so involved with everything else.

My family are my life now and that's all that matters to me. I have no reason to go back to the darker side of my life any more. I love to put my baby in her cot and then wake up in the morning and see her lying there asleep.

I hadn't even listened to my old man. Dad had often warned me that there could be someone better than me out there, to which I usually replied, 'Well, it'd be a fuckin' good fight then, won't it?' But Dad would tell me that having bottle wouldn't be much use to me if I came up against someone tooled up. If they just went BANG! I'd be history.

He had a point.

When you become scared of dying, that's when you can start enjoying life. I can do that now. For 30-odd years I walked a lonely road, but I have a life now. Every morning I wake up and thank God for how grateful I am to be alive. Of course I believe in God. Why else would I have *In God We Trust* tattooed in large letters all the way across my back? It's my cross, my shield. I'm a Catholic, although I haven't been a practising one for years now. I do occasionally go to church. Being a Catholic, I guess it was drummed into me to a point when I was a kid.

Yes, I have faith. I really get the hump when some people ridicule others for their faith, whatever it may be because, if one of them became ill, or someone they cared about became ill, I'm pretty sure they'd go down on their knees and ask God for help. To me though, they're just weekend warriors.

People get it wrong. You don't have to go to church and kneel down in front of Christ. You can say your prayers while you're driving along or walking down the street. It's like having an invisible friend I suppose.

I've already mentioned a mate, Harry Holland. He's a good man, a proper Cockney geezer who greets everyone with the words 'Hello mucker!' I've known Harry for quite a while, since he got close to my brother Freddy in Tenerife. In fact, Harry used to manage Karl Barwise when he was a professional.

Harry hasn't been too well. One day while driving I just said to God, 'Hey mate, do me a favour and keep an eye on Harry will you 'cos he's got family who love him and he's a good guy.' Harry and me often text each other, but when I told him I'd said a prayer for him, he couldn't believe people like me existed.

Bryn's been a bit naughty in the past but now he's seen the light. Nothing wrong with that. Some people, though, have tried to ridicule him for his beliefs and that just makes me very defensive of him. I remember a guy telling me, 'Bryn's gone all holy'. I went mental

246

and asked him why he was taking the piss out of my mate – each to their own.

Bryn holds a lot of prayer meetings. I know some people may be a bit sceptical over things like that, but I do believe because, by rights, I shouldn't even still be here after everything that has happened to me over the years, and I'm praying to God every day. He's obviously got something better planned for me.

People are very cynical in this world nowadays, but I reckon it's always nice to have a bit of faith. It helps you through the day. When I was training with Lenny I didn't feel comfortable talking about these issues because he's very sceptical and I reckoned he'd think I was getting on Bryn's bandwagon. Bryn's really into it. He's a born again Christian. When he talks to you about his faith he does it in such a way that anyone can understand. He reads the scriptures, but in layman's terms.

Vic Dark once told me I shouldn't take things so personally when collecting debts. 'It's a debt, just a job,' he'd told me. He's right of course but, in the case of the fella and his missus who conned my old man out of thousands of pounds, it's so hard to just leave it be. This debt *is* personal and, to tell the truth, it's left me in quite a dilemma. What should I do? Do I go back and serve him up? Think about it. If he hasn't got the money, I've got to hurt him because he's had enough warnings. Or, if hurting him doesn't get results, he's got to disappear.

That's my dilemma from Him up there. He's testing

me all the time. A voice in the back of my mind is telling me to find the guy and to get Dad's money back. To teach the guy a lesson he'll never forget.

That's the Devil talking to me, but Him up there is telling me to rise above it, to leave it be. I'm stuck in the middle. It's so tempting when I need money to think about going after him but, if I do, I'm going to find myself back in that world again and people are going to get badly hurt. Do I really want to risk everything I now have by getting nicked for GBH, attempted murder or kidnapping?

Of course I don't.

But it's a good example of the struggle I'm finding to change my lifestyle. Violence has been part and parcel of my life for so long and has always proved to be an effective way of getting what I want – it's like a drug.

I'd been so proud of myself for staying out of trouble. For two years I hadn't got involved in any violence at all but, not so very long ago, something happened which really upset me. I found myself involved in a fight.

Basically, I was part of a security team at a show. Everything was passing off very smoothly as the evening wore on. I was working alongside the television crew when I became aware of a commotion at the entrance to the venue. One of the security guys who had been working for another company was getting very badly beaten up and, when he hit the floor, five men continued putting in the boot on him, even though he was unconscious. The guys were taking liberties, so me and other security staff raced over to break it up and to rescue our colleague.

By the time we arrived at the scene all hell had broken loose. I delivered a couple of right-handers and smashed up a couple of the guys who were kicking the unconscious doorman. Fortunately, the police were also on hand to help us regain control and the doorman was taken off to hospital.

We'd done a good job in rescuing him but, in the morning, I was feeling really down. If I had been an alcoholic it would be akin to falling off the wagon. I telephoned Bryn to tell him what had happened and how bad I was feeling about it. He reassured me that, as a member of the security team at the event, it had been my job to get involved on this occasion. That's what I had been there for. Anyway, he asked, how could anyone have just stood by while an unconscious man was being kicked by so many others?

Bryn told me he could clearly remember visiting me in the hospital after I'd been attacked in the gym. He'd been there while I was stitched back together again and he told me how much the incident had upset him, Nic and Johnny Fast Hands.

Bryn made me realise that, had the doorman we rescued had a wife and kids, how upset they must be at what had happened to him. At that point I realised that, despite my determination to steer clear of trouble, I'd really had no moral option other than to help the guy out. Who knows, maybe one day the boot will be on the other foot.

Furthermore, in order to justify my actions that night, I remind myself that I had tried to talk to the attackers before letting fly with my fists. I'd tried to calm them down but, as soon as the first punch came in my direction, I just had to fight back.

The incident also showed that I now have a different relationship with the police. We'd been working side by side to sort things out in the foyer that night. Believe it or not, I can actually talk to the police now. In fact, I've got the utmost respect for them – I'm not bootlicking, that's for sure – it's just that I now see them in a different light.

Even when I was arrested in connection with the kidnapping they'd told me not to take things personally, that they were just doing their job. I've come to realise that the only time you should really worry about the police is if you're doing something wrong. Okay, in the past, that's given me plenty of cause for concern but, nowadays, I'm doing my best to stay on the straight and narrow – I've even got an up-to-date tax disc in my car!

Alan Mortlock may be the top promoter of unlicensed boxing, but there's a lot more to him than that. As a youngster, he'd tried to build up a reputation. He was into martial arts and boxing but he also got himself involved in all sorts of trouble and eventually was jailed after attacking a man outside a nightclub. On his release he continued a life of crime, becoming involved in drug dealing and turning to drink.

Alan's life-changing moment occurred in 1991 when he had a 'supernatural' experience and turned to Christianity. He has since formed GodFellas, a play on words from the mob movie *GoodFellas*. Basically, GodFellas is made up of a bunch of lads from Micky Theo's KO Gym who go around prisons to give displays of pad boxing and talk to the inmates. They suggest that, when they are released, the prisoners could pop into the gym to have a work out, maybe even train to be boxers.

Basically, GodFellas is a way of trying to help people while, at the same time, promoting Christianity and trying to channel people's aggressiveness into a more positive direction. It's also a way of saying that, just because you're a boxer, you can still believe in God.

Just as I do.

I've been to a couple of the GodFellas meetings – and also to some Tough Talk meetings given by doormen who have been in prison – guys Alan introduced me to. Tough Talk is run by a couple of guys who run a door security company – all decent work. No shitty nightclubs. They're good men.

One of them, Jeff White, was a champion power lifter for Britain, a real big lump. When I was introduced to him I told him I was pleased to meet him. 'I've heard a lot about you,' he replied.

'Was it all good?' I joked.

'In our eyes, it's all good because we can see through all the bad things.'

The guys from Tough Talk never looked down on me. They were all doormen looking for another chance.

Just like me.

I'm sure God's given me that chance and has always been there to give me a hand up when I really needed it – even though I didn't realise it at the time. I've reached points where my life had meant nothing to me. Points where I felt I couldn't get any lower. Looking back, it's made me realise I shouldn't take anything for granted.

Look where I am now. I might not have every material thing, but I've got a lot more than some people. I've got family who love me, people who like being around me and who I like to be around. That's more than I've had in a long while.

That's not to say Mum and Dad didn't want to be around me, more a case of me not wanting to be around them. I was too self-centred. Too busy doing my own stuff. Too busy focusing on myself. After all the troubles I had to let some people go, despite my feelings of loyalty to some of them if I was to have any chance of retaining my sanity.

Looking back, I felt that by slashing my wrists, I'd shown a weakness but, to be honest, that weakness has become a strength to me. I've realised that what doesn't kill you can make you stronger. I still feel embarrassed about what I did to myself. I look at the marks on my wrists every day. They're a permanent reminder of what I did.

I realise now that alcohol and drugs were just a massive depressant for me and, when I was down, God I was *really* down.

All I want now is for my family to be proud of me. I want my children to love me for the good man I know I can be. I have so much to give and I just hope I've got enough time left for people to see who I really am.

Being so much into music has been an escape at times for me. When some people hear music and songs, that's all they do. I *listen* to it. The words of some songs mean a lot to some people. When a song comes on the radio I always seem to connect it to things that have happened to me in the past so, when I hear Richard Ashcroft's 'The Science of Silence', it reminds me of a particular time in my life. How true some of the words of this song are, and how appropriate they are to my life. They will always remind me of the despair and loneliness, of having to face my fears and having gained strength from others. This will always be mine and Nic's song. Just listening to it inspires me to become a better person.

I have to change for myself as much, if not more, than for anyone else. I can't live a lie any more. But it's not easy and I have experienced setbacks that affect my self-esteem. Sometimes I just feel I'm a complete failure. Sometimes I still get the hump with people. When I do I try to remind myself to look at the scars across my wrists and then I think, no way. Every day I have to look at all the scars all over my body, legacies of the life I've led. That's when I know I *have* to change.

My security work keeps me busy most weekends, and I get occasional labouring jobs. However, I often have a lot of time on my hands during the week. I can earn good money at weekends, but there's no reason not to try to earn more from Monday to Friday. That's why I once decided to visit a local garage to see if they needed anyone to work in their bodyshop. I told the guy there I used to be a paint sprayer and wondered if he had any work he might consider me for. I told him I hadn't worked in a bodyshop for quite a while and that I realised the solvent and paint technology had probably moved on a bit since my time, but that I'd be happy to prepare cars ready for paint and that I reckoned I could be up to the pace in a couple of months.

The guy just looked at me, not saying a word. I got the hump. 'Do you speak English?' I asked.

'Yeah.'

'Well, here's my number, give me a call if there's any work going.'

He just shrugged his shoulders. I felt really dejected. Rejection is always hard to take, but when your self-esteem is low, it's even harder to cope with. I came home, miserable. But Nic was great. She just said, 'Don't worry, we'll be okay. Don't worry about it.'

I have to say that, sometimes, Nic can be as volatile as me. We row but, when things are good, it's just amazing. I've never been with a person who can make me laugh so much, who can pick me up when I'm low.

Since the birth of our baby Annabella I'm shit scared of dying. I want to be there for her. I want to see her make her choices and doing the right thing. I'd like to see her grow up to be a caring young lady who deserves everything I can give her. I want to see her get married, have kids and make me a grandad. How cool would that be? I plan to be the best dad I can for her. I love her with all my heart. As she sleeps I see a small child who is so innocent to the horrible dangers of this dirty world we live in and, yes, to a certain extent, I was a part of that world, but now I'm trying my hardest to be part of the solution.

Her birth has made me see things so differently. I have so much more in my life now and, although at one time, I felt I was unstoppable and was only thinking of myself, I now realise everything could all be taken from me for one reason or another.

Chapter Sixteen

OUT OF THE SHADOWS

I've had to radically rethink the way I've been leading my life. Nowadays, if some guy gives me the hump, I consciously take time to think of the possible repercussions of any action I may take. What if the guy was like me – a father? How would his kids feel if he came home with a black eye or a broken jaw? Now I prefer to just walk away from situations – let them have a nice day – because it wouldn't be much fun for their family to watch them drink their dinner through a straw.

That brings me to a situation a few years back which, if I could turn back the clock, I most certainly would.

One of my deeds that I probably regret more than any other.

Big John, Johnny Fast Hands, another colleague we called Boothy and I, were running a door in a little nearby town. I was never a head doorman, I was more a battleship. If the head doorman couldn't handle the situation he found himself in, they'd call for me. I guess I was a bit like the gimp in the movie *Pulp Fiction* – perhaps they thought there was little point in talking to some people for ages when it's obvious a good right-hander will sort everything out. We were all working alongside another couple of doormen, who turned out to be right dogs.

You're often tested when you're new faces at a fresh door – that's pretty normal – and we dealt with anything that came at us. Some of the arseholes in the area did their level best but failed to push their weight around on our door. Normally, we'd let people in because, if you've got a good team on the door, it doesn't matter too much who comes in because you should always be able to deal with them. I'm not saying we were supermen but, any doormen reading this will know what I mean, once they got to know us we never used to get too much aggro with people and, in fact, we became reasonably friendly with most of them in this particular club. It's a bit like the saying: keep your friends close, but your enemies closer.

That worked in our favour. If ever there was trouble and we were outnumbered, we usually could rely on some back-up from the more regular punters which isn't such a bad thing in certain situations.

Before long we had this club running pretty well –

no aggro, better people coming in, and a smarter dress code. We'd turned it right around. After all, who'd want to go to a club where people were just out looking for aggro? Once people knew it wasn't like that any more, the place just got better and better.

We usually worked Friday, Saturday and Sunday nights. One Sunday, just as we were leaving, the manager called a meeting. He told us it would only take five minutes. We went upstairs where he told us that the club would be closing down for a while, saying there'd be some refurbishment undertaken. Although we couldn't think why they needed to bother, after all, why fix something that isn't broken, we never suspected anything could be different than had been explained to us.

A week later we found work at another club, no problem. Then Big John phoned me. He was going mad. Apparently, the club hadn't shut down at all. The two pricks who had been working alongside us were, in fact, running the door at that very moment, which, we thought, was a proper liberty.

What was happening, isn't so unusual. Clubs get the heavy squads in until they get the doors working efficiently, then replace them with less qualified staff and pay them peanuts. Pay peanuts, get monkeys.

The two Johns, Boothy and me, were not too happy about the way things had turned out and decided to go back to the club for a chat the following Friday. As we drove past the club we spotted the two pricks standing there, along with two big black guys and another geezer. Mind you, you should have seen their faces when the pricks spotted us driving slowly past! What a treat!

We parked up. As we got out of the car we noticed the pricks hurriedly talking to their new colleagues before they quickly disappeared inside. The remaining doormen waited for us. They stood in front of the door. 'Not tonight lads, you're barred,' said one of them. 'What the fuck for?' I asked. By now I really had the hump but, although Big John and Johnny Fast Hands really wanted to smash them up I, for once, remained calm. I suggested to one of the black doormen that he came around the corner with me for a chat and, to give him his dues, he did.

Everyone thought we'd be having 'a straightener' but, as soon as we got around the corner, the guy said: 'Listen Dom, we don't want any trouble, we're just doing our jobs.' To be honest, I was a little taken aback. Having listened to him, I realised he was right. They had got the call after we'd left the job and he'd been told we'd left because we'd found work at another club and that the two pricks we'd left behind had been our bosses! I have to admit, I found that rather amusing. The pricks had trouble tying their own laces, let alone running a door!

Bottom line was, we had a chat and worked things out. As it happened, the club we'd moved on to was closer to home and the money was better so we weren't really losing out financially. But we didn't want to let this other team start to think they'd taken the door from us – any doormen would understand that point of view. We told them we'd got the place sorted and that our presence had been required elsewhere.

That said, we knew we'd have to speak to the two pricks. If they thought they'd got one over on us, they'd soon find out they hadn't. We sent one of the doormen into the club to look for them but, it appears, they'd already left the club by the back door – supposedly, they were suddenly needed at another venue. Bullshit!

To say we were a bit pissed off was an understatement, but we went on our way. I have to say though, our 'replacements' were a great bunch of lads and, since then, we've even worked together at bigger events. I guess it sometimes works out better not to go in all guns blazing.

We'd only been driving for around five minutes when Johnny Fast Hands received a telephone call from one of the pricks saying he was sorry and that they didn't want any trouble. Johnny was yelling back at him; in fact me and Big John thought we'd become deaf by the time he got off the phone! 'That fuckin' told him!' he said. Big John and me just looked at each other and started laughing. We decided this problem required the 'personal touch' and made plans to go to the pricks' homes on the following Sunday. Just imagine, they'd be sitting down, tucking into their Sunday roasts when us four all turn up with the hump. That would give them indigestion! But it never happened. Somehow, they got wind of it and were not at home – all day and night.

On the Monday, Johnny received another telephone call from one of the pricks. We should leave them alone he said, else they'd go to the Old Bill to get us nicked. Told you they were dogs. Then the other telephoned. He was sorry. He didn't want any more trouble and, if we agreed to leave him alone, he and his fellow prick would leave the door and never go back there.

The following Saturday, I got a call from the head doorman asking to see me. I didn't know quite what to expect, but the four of us all went together. By now, I'd got to know one of the black guys, Tony, and I could tell as soon as I saw the big grin on his face that all was cool. He had a handful of money. 'Thanks Dom,' he said as he handed me the cash. There I was, expecting to have a good old punch up and Tony was handing over what was a kind of out of court settlement! So, the story ended on a good note. The pricks had done the right thing. They'd rung the new door team and told them they were leaving with some excuse about getting extra money and an easier job elsewhere, and that they were welcome to continue working the door on their own. That suited Tony. Now he had his own door and was getting paid better as the money was now going directly to him. With that, he gave us a drink as a sort of pay off, saying he reckoned the pricks had been right dogs and thanking us for being gents.

After splitting the money, Big John and me had enough cash to pay for flights to Spain for a week's break, so it all worked out pretty well in the end.

Or so I thought.

It was probably around a year later that Big John and me decided to visit my Dad. En-route we decided to pop in to see a friend of mine at his office. It was a lovely day, blue skies and so on but, after we'd seen my pal and were driving out of the car park, I had to give way to a large people carrier – a flashy seven-seater – and driving it was one of the pricks who'd conned us out of the door work. Big John told me to leave it but, me being me, I just couldn't do that.

I jumped out of the car and marched over to the people carrier. The prick hadn't even noticed me as he got out to open the doors for his passengers. As the last person was getting out of his motor he caught sight of me out of the corner of his eye and he could tell straight away that I wasn't happy to see him. He tried to calm the situation down, asking me how my boxing was going, saying he'd watched me on the telly, but I was having none of it.

I told him we had unfinished business to sort out. The moment in my life that, more than most, I so wish I could take back. The guy (please note I'm not referring to him now as a prick) realised what was about to happen. Whatever he was going to say to me was not going to make any difference. He had tears in his eyes and started going on about having heart problems – but what I remember most of all is

263

how he started saying how much he'd changed. 'Dom, I don't do that sort of work any more. I drive business people around. *I've got a baby girl.* I'm a different man today!'

He was pleading with me in front of his passengers but it didn't matter a jot to me. I wanted him to pay for losing us work at that stupid door.

Better still, I had an audience so I *had* to perform, like a true entertainer.

As he apologised again, I nutted him. CRACK! Down the side of his vehicle he slid. I just looked down at him with contempt, then told his watching passengers that, if he'd been supposed to be looking after them, they should get someone better.

I walked back to my car. Big John gave me one of his hard looks. 'Feel better now, do you?' he said. 'You'll regret that.'

And, hand on heart, I really do.

Okay, the guy had done me a wrong in the past, but he'd apologised, even begged to me in front of his people, but I just wouldn't let it go. Who gave me the right to be judge and juror?

To this day, I really beat myself up over what happened that day. I was so wrong. When I think now about what he told me, that he had a baby – how could I have done what I did? I'd wanted people's respect, even to be feared, but now I just look back at myself with shame. I'd become as bad, even worse, than him. What I'd done to him was far worse than anything he'd ever done to me.

I'm not going to name the guy – and I know it's unlikely he'll ever pick up this book but, just in case he does, please believe me, I'm so sorry for what I did to you. The pain and embarrassment I caused you that day will always stay with me. I'm so ashamed of what I did to you and I pray that you and your family are blessed in ways I don't deserve to be.

God bless you and your family.

This episode has also taught me another important lesson. Despite the guy insisting he had changed, I still attacked him. Which raises certain possibilities.

After all, what am I saying now? I'm telling you that *I've* changed – but that doesn't mean that everyone else has – people I've upset or hurt in the past. As I wrote earlier, I can't now assume that just because my life is now so much more orderly that there aren't still people out there who would want to get even with me, can I?

And, even though I've got wiser, it doesn't mean that if I'm backed up against a wall, I won't come out fighting.

When it was my Dad's birthday on 26 November, Nic and I went to put some flowers on his grave. Later that day I was sitting with the baby and a song came on the radio – 'The Living Years' by Mike and the Mechanics – with the line about his dad dying and him not being there. Nic saw the look on my face. 'I don't half miss the old cunt,' I said. Now I know that's not a nice word to describe my Dad but anybody who knows me, and how I was with my Dad, it was rarely,

'Hello Dad', it was usually, 'Hello you old wanker' or something like that. That was our sort of humour. If ever I rang and said, 'Hello Dad' he'd want to know what was wrong.

I remember when I legged it to Tenerife while I was on bail. I rang a few trusted friends to let them know what was going on. I rang Matty to say thanks for everything he'd done for me. Then I rang my Dad. I was crying my eyes out. 'Dad, I love ya,' I said.

'I love you too,' he replied. 'What's the matter, where are you?'

I told him I was on my way to Freddy's in Tenerife, but he wasn't to tell anyone. I knew I could trust Dad, he was always so loyal. I reckon that's where I got it from.

If I could be half the father he was to Freddy and me, I'll have it sussed. It hurts me so much that he never got to see our Annabella. I was so proud to have him as a father. I just keep thinking how much it would mean to me that my Dad would be just as proud of me. The things he told me, warned me about – yet, when I was younger, so often all I could think was, 'yeah, yeah, get a life you boring old git'.

As I've got older – dare I say matured – I realise people like my Dad had lived their lives and had already made their mistakes. Dad was just passing on the benefit of his experiences down to Freddy and me. He'd been there. He'd done that. We should have listened to him more. But we thought we already knew it all. How wrong could we have been? Dad always told me the truth. He wasn't trying to be boring. By not listening to him as often as I should, I had to find out a lot of things the hard way. I made so many mistakes.

A couple of years before Dad died, I visited him at his mobile home in Jaywick. It was the only time I ever stayed overnight at his place. We sat up chatting together for ages. At one point I said to him, 'I'm so sorry Dad.'

'What for?'

'I fucked up.'

'You ain't fucked up,' he replied, 'you've been all around the world!'

Dad was great. A man of proper morals. Unlike me, he never broke the law in his life and he was as straight as the day is long. He worked from the age of 15 until he was 68, and he did it all for us – his family.

Okay, there was never a great deal of money, but we had a good life as kids. It's such a shame because, when I did have a bit of cash in my pockets, I often offered to take Dad away on trips – Spain, America and so on – but, by this time, he was in a wheelchair and he didn't fancy going on long journeys.

Although I often visited him, Dad reckoned I'd only telephone him if I was abroad. Once I called him from New York, the next week it was from Chicago, after that it was Thailand and then Spain. It was 6am American time when I called Dad from Times Square in New York. I was with Enzo, Nick Cole and Enzo's boy Michael.

'Where are you?' Dad asked.

'Times Square.'

'Bloody hell, you get about!'

When I apologised to Dad for all my mistakes he chose to remind me that I was a lucky man. Lucky because I'd done things he could only dream about, and that I'd been around the world and visited places he had never had the chance to see. All my mates loved Dad. Even when I wasn't around, they'd pop in and visit him when he was living in Woodford.

I remember him asking why I never brought birds home, but I could never see the point as I rarely went out with the same one for long. Like that, he'd have met a different girl every week!

Dad was 76 when he moved into his mobile home soon after his and Mum's marriage ended. It was two days after the Chris Henry contest, so I wasn't in the happiest frame of mind when Long-haired John and I drove him down to Jaywick. I felt so bad seeing Dad in that place. He seemed so lonely and, as we left him, I remember really hating the fact we had to leave him behind.

Even now, I miss him so much.

I've seen life on both sides now and it's brought everything home to me and has shown me what means the most to me. I just thank Him upstairs that I've never been banged up. I guess He's just got better plans for me.

I realise now who my real friends are. I know who I can trust. I'm very lucky because there are a lot of people out there who would, I know, do anything for me. On the other hand, there are people out there I thought were my friends, but they're not.

It's all very well for people who've got pots of money because they can afford to give you, maybe 50 or a hundred quid but, if they're prepared to stand side by side with you in a ruck, that's completely different. People like Johnny Fast Hands or Bryn, Paul, Vic Dark or another good mate, Henry Smith. They'd do anything for me. They're so loyal. You could go to war with guys like that at your side. Me? My loyalty is undivided. As Johnny Fast Hands would say, 'Even if you were wrong, I'd still make you right.'

I used to drive a lorry for Henry, who runs a legitimate furniture business. Nowadays, he's also into property development, big time. Yes, Henry's done very well for himself and he's been a wonderful and supportive friend to me. In fact, he's put a lot of work my way and he's 100 per cent straight. At one time I used to help set up exhibitions for him and his dad, who I call H. I've known them both for years. They're such good men. Henry's always looked after me. He even offered to buy me a brand new Mercedes car so I could have a go at chauffeuring. He just wanted me to do better for myself. I owe him so much. In fact, he hasn't a clue how much! Henry, like Bryn, deserves so much more than I could ever give them.

Only recently, as I was making my way to Henry's building site, I was thinking how cool is this – going out to work! After all my shady dealings, I can't tell you how good it feels to be going out in the morning to do a decent day's work for a decent day's pay alongside decent people – and not need to look over my shoulder to see if the Old Bill are around. I get the train and work from 9am to 5pm on the site and never need to get up to anything naughty – brilliant! No doubt about it though, it's hard work, but the people I work with are great. They all earn their money then go home. It's so uncomplicated. It's really opened my eyes to the real world.

When I look back at some of the more unsavoury characters I've worked alongside – people whose dirty work I've been doing – I can't help feeling so glad to have left that world behind me. I've wasted so much time building a reputation as a hard man, but it was all a load of old bollocks.

I need more direction in my life. Although labouring is fine for me at this time in my life, it's not something I could do long term. I want to improve myself. Money's not the be-all and end-all. Whenever I have had a pocketful of money, I've tended to share it out with friends. But I do need a job with a degree of stability to it. I need a future. I need a trade. I'd like to settle down and get married. Nothing flash. And I need to start thinking about a pension.

I have a diploma in personal training to fall back on, which means I'm qualified to take fitness classes. With my background, that would be a possibility but, to be honest, it's not really a line of work I really want to get into. Okay, it's good money, and a lot of people say they'd really like me to train them, probably because of who I am, but I don't think I'd want to handle all the messing about that goes with it. So often I've seen people really keen to get fit and turning up at the gym three or four times a week but, before long, the hard work dulls their enthusiasm and that's when all the excuses come trotting out. They'd be wasting my time and theirs.

As things stand, I'm just living for the moment, working as much as I can. Look, I'm 36 and, to be honest, at one time I could never have predicted still being around at this age. I remember going to Brighton with a group of friends to celebrate my 30th birthday. We had such a laugh – a brilliant time. But I can still remember telling them how I couldn't believe I'd reached the big three-o. Well, look at me now. Although I've been incredibly lucky at least once – I'm still here!

I have to say, I sometimes think the future's scary. What will I be like if I get to 60? Some doors open, others close. Hopefully, one or two will open up just for me. Who knows? I'm so glad certain people, great people, have stuck by me and helped me when I was on my knees, when my head was messed up with drink and drugs. But I can't help feeling some people threw me overboard, so-called mates who didn't stay the course. In fact, some treated me like I was a leper.

I believe the truth will set me free. I've lived a life that some people would never believe or understand. So much pain. So much violence. I was a man lost, in search of things I wasn't meant to have – not at that point in my life anyway. Until recently, my life had been wasted. A waste of money, sweat, tears and negative energy. Luckily for me, things have changed, and all for the better. All I ever wanted was to be loved. To be part of a family – a family where it didn't matter if you cried in front of one another or just sat together having a laugh.

I have that now. I've got the most amazing child, a wicked woman in every sense of the word, and a great step-daughter. My children will never be like me – I'll make sure of that, whatever it takes.

We live our lives by our own mistakes and, needless to say, I made more than most. I lived my life using my past as an excuse, but how long could that have continued? Life is not a game. It's not them (the police) or us. It's not about winning or losing. It's about enjoying life.

It sounds daft, but I reckon I needed that attack in the gym to make me see the light. Had it not been for that I would either have ended up in prison, or dead – and I didn't fancy either option. Nowadays, when I step outside, no matter how foul the weather is, it's a lovely day – it's just that we don't always realise it. I really needed that good kick up the arse to slow me down because I'd become someone that I'd always fought against – a bully! As a result, in spite of all the recognition I received as a world champion boxer, I guess I'll always be more infamous than famous.

I've learnt my lessons but I've had to do it the hard way. I'm wiser now. Before I snap I find myself having to justify any possible act of violence. I truly believe now that it could only happen if someone was to do something against my family – and no-one with any sense would want to risk putting themselves in that position.

But it's not easy. I really am trying to talk things over more and trying to slow things down a bit. After a lifetime of life in the fast lane, all I want now is to be normal but, looking around the world we live in, can anyone really tell me what normal is?

I'm not perfect and never will be. Show me a person who says he or she is, and I'll show you a liar, but no matter how much I'm now trying to be a better person, I can never turn back the clock. I can't undo the things I've done.

But that's in the past. Now I'm living my life out of the shadows. Now I can look at myself in the mirror and be 90 per cent happy with what I see.

At least these days I can sleep at night. I now realise that those who pretend to be something they are not always get found out in the end. In this life you can lie to everyone else, but not to yourself. Look into your own eyes and you can see the truth because, as they so rightly say, your eyes are the windows to your soul.

No doubt about it, I've been a really bad person but I'm hoping that by putting pen to paper, at the end of my story, not just you but *I* will understand why I did the things I did.

DOMINIC NEGUS: BOXING STATISTICS

Amateur career:

Top 10 rated amateur heavyweight

34 contests, won 23

North East Divisional Finals winner 1994, 1995

Professional career:

19 contests Won 13 (6 KOs) Lost 5 Drawn 1

Date	Opponent	Location	Result
3/9/1996	Gareth Thomas	London	W TKO 2
28/9/1996	Patrick Lawrence	Barking	W TKO 2
11/1/1997	Naveed Anwar	Barking	W RTD 2
4/3/1997	Nigel Rafferty	London	W pts 4
20/5/1997	Nigel Rafferty	London	W pts 4
17/6/1997	Chris Henry	Cheshunt	W TKO 10

British (Southern Area) Cruiserweight title

Date	Opponent	Location	Result
2/9/1997	Trevor Small	London	D Pts 8
11/11/1997	Konstantin Ochrej	London	W KO 6

21/4/1997	Bruce Scott	London	L TKO 9
	British (Southern Area) Cruiserweight title		

22/10/1998	Kevin Mitchell	Barking	L RTD 5
18/2/1999	Kevin Mitchell	Barking	W Pts 10
	Vacant British (Southern Area) Cruiserweight title		

13/9/1999	Chris Woollas	London	W Pts 10
8/9/2000	Tony Booth	Bristol	L Pts 6
6/10/2000	Garry Delaney	Maidstone	L Pts 10
	British (Southern Area) Cruiserweight title		

26/5/2001	Paul Fiske	London	W TKO 1
29/9/2001	Eamonn Glennon	London	W Pts 6
8/12/2001	Eddie Knight	Dagenham	W KO 2
	WBU Inter Continental Super Cruiserweight title		

26/1/2002	Paul Bonson	London	W Pts 4
10/7/2002	Audley Harrison	London	L Pts 6

Unlicensed career:

10 contests, won 9, lost 1

	Roger Toon	Purfleet	W Pts 6
	Paul Somerfield	Purfleet	W TKO 3
	Karl Barwise	Purfleet	L Pts 6
	Ginger Hooper	Purfleet	W TKO 1
	Harry van der Meer	Purfleet	W Pts 6
	'The Russian'	Enfield	W TKO 1
	Nicholai	Purfleet	W Pts 6
	John Sheridan	Clacton	W TKO 2
28/11/2005	Jeff Temperley	Purfleet	W TKO 5
	IBA World Heavyweight title		

9/12/2005	Karl Barwise	Purfleet	W TKO 2
	Roy Shaw title		

ACKNOWLEDGEMENTS

Maybe you are either a bit like me in that you sometimes read the end of the book first of all, or you've stuck at it and read it right through. Either way, you've got this far. Well, it took me and my good friend and confidant a while to put pen to paper. The man behind the pen is one Ivan Sage, a man who has known me for a good while and, over the time putting this book together we have become good friends. I've been blessed to have met this man. Some people wouldn't have touched this book with a bargepole but, after talking to me, Ivan realised that there was more to me than just the stories he had heard. For that alone, I must say a big thank you.

But there are so many more people I should acknowledge for their love and support over the years, some I may not have even seen for a very long time, and

I must apologise if there are some I have inadvertently not mentioned. So here goes:

First off the blocks, my biggest thank you must go to my Nic. What a lady. She has stood by me through thick and thin. Even when the shit was hitting the fan, she was there for me. We may have our ups and downs, but there is no way I would change her – not even for a million quid. Hold on, did I say a million quid? Only joking! Nic, I love you and the girls so much. Thanks for making my life complete.

Nic's family took me for who I am, not what they had heard about me. Nic's mum Lorraine and stepdad John are so cool. Lorraine, or Mum as I call her, is great, so open-minded and never takes sides. If we have problems she is the first person we turn to. John, quite a quiet man, is a great man to have around and always offers sound advice. As for Nic's brothers, we all get on like a house on fire and, when we get together, it always turns out to be a great day.

I mustn't forget my own Mum either – she'd do her nut if I did! – she looked after me and Freddy, kept us fed, clean and brought us up the right way and I love her so much for that. Mum, I love you lots.

Thanks also to Dad – even though he isn't around any more. What a man. I miss him every day and not a single day passes that I haven't thought of him. I just wish he could have lived to see Annabella. I know he would have been so proud of her and my family. He wasn't just my Dad. He was my best mate. We had no

Acknowledgements

secrets. I like to think he would be proud of me, not for my past, but for my future. He would have loved Nic. I just so wish he could have seen how much my life has changed. Dad, I love you mate!

To my brother Freddy, niece Boo, and nephew Dude, thank you for your support. I won't forget it. I love you all.

To my brother in arms, Bryn. The Man Upstairs had it planned that I should meet Bryn. He's stood by me, stuck his neck on the line for me when others left me. Bryn is a true friend. Never afraid to tell me when I'm wrong. Bryn, I love you like a brother.

Ambrose Mendy, you are the guy who first suggested I write this book. Thanks.

Vic Dark, what a fella to have on your side. This man is fearless. He doesn't know what a backward step is. Thanks for taking me along with you Vic. We've had some of the best times.

Colin and Maureen Cordingley are great people. Colin was there for me when I was a kid, and he's still there for me now.

Ray Coleman, Sarah and their family. They only want good things for me and my family. They just want us to be happy and, at the moment, we are. Ray also sponsored me while I was boxing, as did Chris and Andrea Smith. Thank you so much.

Henry Smith, his dad H, and the rest of his family. H has always been good to me and gave me work when others wouldn't. He always took me on my word which is a big thing nowadays. When the shit started

279

flying in my life Henry made me sit down with his dad, and what a lot of sense he made me see that day. Thanks for your time H. You're a top man.

Long-haired John. You're the most calming influence. Another man I owe so much to, who's always been there for me.

Matty Austin Cooper. When you opened the door to me early that morning, you were like an angel sent down to show me the way. I hadn't seen you for years, yet you took me in, cooked me breakfast and gave me the keys to your flat. Fuck me, you don't get many friends like that!

Brian from Woodford, thanks for having time for me while I was having all that aggro.

Wayne Cummings, you've been a good friend. Thanks for everything – and I'm so sorry for what you had to see.

Enzo, my old friend, how many times have I slept on your sofa? At times you were just as lost as me. We were like two men stuck on a raft out to sea in gale force winds, both of us just holding on for dear life but, hey, we're still here.

Danny the Mex and his dad The Fox. Great mates. We've had some great times and laughs. Being with them was like being out with my own family.

Phil Soundy, you gave me back my faith in men. You're a real gent.

Ronnie and Carrie Nash, I guess I was meant to meet you both. All I can say to Ron is 'bumgravy'. (Private joke.)

Acknowledgements

Joe Egan. This man alone could take on an army on just his heart. Joe, you're a man's man, a true gent. You've been brought up well and you know the meaning of loyalty. In your birthplace of Ireland you were, and still are, one of the best fighters to come out of the amateur rankings. You're a true friend. God bless you and your family big man!

God bless also to Roy Shaw, a legend in his own right. Another true warrior who came up the hard way and asked for no favours from anyone. I grew up looking up to men like you Roy. You were one of my heroes and now, on top of that, you're a friend.

Unlicensed boxing promoter Alan Mortlock, you took me on when others wouldn't. You, Laura and the boys brought me a ray of light and have been there for me. Thanks mate.

Gary and Danny Bedford, you never let stories about me get to you. We came, we fought, and we overcame. You helped me exorcise the demons that had played havoc in my head for years. Now I can walk away from the sport I loved with full closure.

Trainers Lee Ottey and Pat Sandy, thank you.

Darren Jones and his girlfriend Sue have come to all of my fights. So has Mick from the David Lloyd Centre. They are true supporters and nice people.

My former manager Dave Lewis. Dave, you are one of my 'nicer' friends!

Jeff, Micky and new addition Harrison, thanks for the times you let me kip on your sofa.

Young George (aka Skippy), you're a good man but

now you're living in Australia. Hurry home mate and help me sell this book!

Big John and Johnny Fast Hands, it was always a privilege to work with you. Big Dave, Kevin the Potato Head and Paul Biggs, the same goes for you too, and thanks to Ian McAllister for giving us work when we didn't have any.

I haven't seen The Tall Fella for some time but I won't forget him or his mum and nan who, after letting me sleep on their couch overnight, ended up with me staying with them for nearly a year!

Paul 'Fozzy' Foster, you're a crazy dude, and a good mate, and Neil, Alan the Hairdresser and Tan and Teeth, you're all great guys to go out with. Para Paul, one of our true fighters for our country, you're a top man and a nice guy.

Ginger Nick and his mum and dad Jackie and Bill, you are all one-offs. You bent over backwards to help me when I was going through my troubles and I won't forget it.

Wolfie, you're a great little fighter and the sky's the limit if you do the right thing.

There are so many others I should thank for their friendship, including Cod (before you ask, it's because he drinks like a fish!), ring whip Ernie Draper, Jason Guiver – a very underrated boxer on the unlicensed circuit, Paul King, Roy Hilder, Martin and Tony Bowers, Steve Bunce, Tony Darke, Harry Holland, 'TV' Dave, Garry Delaney, John Cronie and his family, Steve Hurricks and his family, Terry Sabine and

Acknowledgements

Debbie, Carlton Leach, Matty, Gary Gordon and the boys at KO Gym, Noel T, Micky Theo, Lee Chisholm, Warren and all the guys from the David Lloyd Centre.

Best wishes to Jason Burton, aka Butnuts. Not telling you what that means. That's between him and my brother!

And last, but by no means least, some good news that occurred just in time to be included in this book. Although my former trainer Lenny Butcher no longer wanted anything more to do with me, I still wanted to record my appreciation for all he had done for me. Readers will be aware that, despite everything that happened between us, I remained very fond of Lenny and fully understood why he felt the way he did. My original acknowledgement to Lenny read as follows: 'Lenny Butcher, I owe you such a lot, even though it seems we've burnt our bridges. I miss you. You and Laurie made me feel like one of the family.'

While I was working as part of a security team at a boxing bill in Dagenham in July 2006, I saw Lenny. At the time he was working with one of his protégés, Richard Horton. After Richard's contest I followed them back to the dressing room hoping, but not expecting, Lenny would forgive me.

Thankfully, he did.